Date: _1-6-01 Spiritual_

Speaker: _GJHS_

Title of Message: _Soar with your Strengths_

Judges 6 -12

Key Verses:

MATT 24-3 - MATT 25-14-15 1 Peter 4-10

---

① Everyone has A Gift
② Each person responsible to manage Gift
③ Gift brings Strength and Energy

How to recognize Swaps to Identify Gifts
① YEARNING of the heart - Thats for me desire
② SAtisfaction - Pleasure each Time you Perform
   this thing you-do -
③ Rapid Learning in your Gift - taking Place
④ while performing Activity there were Glimpses
   of Excellence
⑤ Continual Improvement - getting better

Notes:

Romans 12:2

DISCOVER YOUR DESTINY

DISCOVER YOUR Destiny

BILL & KATHY PEEL

FINDING

THE COURAGE

TO FOLLOW

YOUR DREAMS

NAVPRESS

BRINGING TRUTH TO LIFE

P.O. Box 35001, Colorado Springs, Colorado 80935

The Navigators is an international Christian organization. Our mission is to reach, disciple, and equip people to know Christ and to make Him known through successive generations. We envision multitudes of diverse people in the United States and every other nation who have a passionate love for Christ, live a lifestyle of sharing Christ's love, and multiply spiritual laborers among those without Christ.

NavPress is the publishing ministry of The Navigators. NavPress publications help believers learn biblical truth and apply what they learn to their lives and ministries. Our mission is to stimulate spiritual formation among our readers.

© 1996 by William Carr Peel and Kathy Peel
All rights reserved. No part of this publication may be reproduced in any form without written permission from NavPress, P.O. Box 35001, Colorado Springs, CO 80935.
www.navpress.com
Library of Congress Catalog Card Number: 96-43266
ISBN 08910-99832

Front cover photo: Tony Stone Images
Back cover photo: Matthew Barnes

Some of the anecdotal illustrations in this book are true to life and are included with the permission of the persons involved. All other illustrations are composites of real situations, and any resemblance to people living or dead is coincidental.

Unless otherwise identified, all Scripture quotations in this publication are taken from the *HOLY BIBLE: NEW INTERNATIONAL VERSION* ® (NIV®). Copyright © 1973, 1978, 1984 by International Bible Society. Used by permission of Zondervan Publishing House. All rights reserved. Other versions used include: the *New American Standard Bible* (NASB), © The Lockman Foundation 1960, 1962, 1963, 1968, 1971, 1972, 1973, 1975, 1977; *The Message: New Testament with Psalms and Proverbs* by Eugene H. Peterson, copyright © 1993, 1994, 1995, used by permission of NavPress Publishing Group; the *Revised Standard Version Bible* (RSV), copyright 1946, 1952, 1971, by the Division of Christian Education of the National Council of the Churches of Christ in the USA, used by permission, all rights reserved; *The Living Bible* (TLB), © 1971 owned by assignment by the Illinois Regional Bank N.A. (as trustee), used by permission of Tyndale House Publishers, Inc., Wheaton, IL 60189; the *Amplified New Testament* (AMP), © The Lockman Foundation 1954, 1958; and the *King James Version* (KJV).

Peel, William Carr.
    Discover your destiny : finding the courage to follow your dreams /
    Bill and Kathy Peel.
           p.   cm.
      ISBN 0-89109-983-2
      1. Bible. O.T. Nehemiah—Devotional literature.   2. Dreams in the Bible.
    3. Dreams—Religious aspects—Christianity.   4. Vocation—Christianity.   I. Peel, Kathy,
    1951–   . II. Title.
    BS1365.4.P44   1996
    248.4—dc20   96-43266
                                                      CIP

Printed in the United States of America

2 3 4 5 6 7 8 9 10 11 12 13 14 15 / 10 09 08 07 06 05 04 03 02 01

FOR A FREE CATALOG OF
NAVPRESS BOOKS & BIBLE STUDIES,
CALL 1-800-366-7788 (USA)
or 1-416-499-4615 (CANADA)

Contents

If everyone had an encouraging, energetic,
and enthusiastic friend like Dan Johnson, more dreams
would be followed, more destinies discovered.
We dedicate this book to him.

It takes many people to take a dream and make it into a book. First, we would like to thank our children, John, Joel and James Peel—the Peel dream team.

A special thanks to Steve Webb, John Eames, Kent Hughes, Paul Santhouse, Nancy McAlister, Donna Thurman, and the whole NavPress team.

If it weren't for Jan Johnson and Holly Halverson, editors par excellence, this book would probably still be piles of papers on our office floor. Kathy Mitchell and Katie Weiss helped a great deal as well.

Finally, a big thank-you goes to the Queen of Make It Happen and second most important woman in Bill Peel's life—Nancy Guthrie.

God's Whisper

*You've got to believe deep inside
yourself that you're destined
to do great things.*

JOE PATERNO, COLLEGE FOOTBALL COACH

*What makes life dreary
is the want of a motive.*

GEORGE ELIOT, ENGLISH NOVELIST, 1815–1880

Discovering your destiny. That's what this book is about. But even more, it's about getting to know the One behind your destiny, the God who created you with a purpose in mind. It's about tuning your heart to listen to His softest whisper and becoming alert to His cues and intimations. In order to do this, we're going to look at your dreams and desires; study them in light of the skills, talents, and resources God has given you; and evaluate them against the standard of Scripture.

To keep our feet grounded in the reality of God's Word, we'll look at the life of Nehemiah, a man who had a grand dream to rebuild the city of Jerusalem, which had lain in ruins all his life. His dream must have seemed irrational considering his circumstances, but it was his destiny, and he lived to see it become a reality. There's much we can learn and apply to our own circumstances from Nehemiah: how he heard God's whisper; how he dreamed, prepared, prayed, and planned; how he worked with other people to bring about his dream; and how he stayed focused on it.

> There is nothing like a dream to create the future.
>
> —VICTOR HUGO, FRENCH POET

Over the last twenty-five years we've worked with thousands of men and women—in corporations, churches, communities, families—who are trying to make some sense of their lives. Many of these men and women have been frustrated, tired, unfulfilled, and bored. They wonder why they're alive and what they're supposed to be doing. We've wondered this ourselves and, in our own searching and that of others, we've made three observations:

> ⟶ As human beings we all long to be fulfilled and feel like our lives matter. We want to know our purpose.

> ⟶ We are more interested in finding out the reason for which our Creator created us than in getting to know our Creator.

➠Because of this misplaced focus, most of us live in the foggy recess of our potential, frustrated over what might have been or could be.

Bob sat in his leather chair and spoke more honestly than maybe he'd spoken in his entire life.

"Okay. I made it to the top. I'm president of my own company. Business is great. My family has everything they need—or I guess they do. Does it matter to my wife that I hate to go to the office every morning? Does it matter to my kids that their father works twelve hours a day and is frequently in a bad mood? Maybe as long as they have the house, cars, clothes, jewelry, toys, and trips, it really doesn't matter. Yeah, I suppose they have what they need.

> We should all be concerned about the future because we will have to spend the rest of our lives there.
>
> —CHARLES KETTERING,
> AMERICAN INVENTOR

"But does it matter whether or not I have what *I* need? Do I ever get to stop long enough to do something *I* want to do? I've always dreamed of training for a marathon. I want to start a camp for inner-city children, and I'd like to take a photography class. I've got some dreams buried deep inside me. Does that matter?"

Does God care if Bob runs in a marathon, starts a camp, or takes great pictures?

We believe that God does care and that our dreams do matter, and we also believe that many times our dreams offer a clue to our God-given purpose in life. Not that there's a tried-and-true equation for discovering God's will or a Web site you can log onto or a personality inventory test you can take. It's not quite that simple. But neither is it as mysterious as some think. If we were honest, we'd admit that much of the mystery surrounding our destiny is a result of our own fear of knowing God's will and surrendering ourselves to Him. We're afraid He'll make us do something we hate or send us someplace we don't want to go—and we'll be miserable. Actually, nothing could be further from the truth. Think about it. Do you think God will call you to open a restaurant if your kids put the poison control number on autodial? We don't think so. Or do you suppose that God will make you become a bank teller when your idea of a balanced checkbook is coming within one hundred dollars — give or take — of the bank's balance? Doubtful. Or if you can think of few things worse than spending time with people, one-on-one, listening to their problems, do you think God will guide you to become a counselor? It's not likely.

On the other hand, if you get a rush from thinking about influencing the minds of young children and stay awake at night thinking of creative ways to teach history or literature, is it possible that God might open a door for you to do just that? Yes it is. Or if you love to travel and experience different cultures, could He have possibly designed you with this bent because He wants you to do this on a regular basis? He surely could have. Or if you feel exhilarated when you hit a golf ball three hundred yards, straight down the fairway, do you think you might have this ability for a reason? We think you should entertain this as a serious possibility.

We believe our God-given destiny is also where our deepest joy lies, not in the opposite direction of our desires — unless, of course, they are sinful. And that's a significant part of discovering our destiny — learning to discern our motives, which ones are good and honorable and which ones are sinful. God has given us guidelines in Scripture, such as the Ten Commandments. No gray areas there. If you're dreaming of stealing half a million dollars to start a missionary agency, you can be sure that's not God's will. If you have a "spiritual" experience in bed with someone other than your spouse and dream of starting a new life together (present family not included), as one man and woman told us they dreamed of, you may have had a spiritual experience, but it certainly wasn't from God's Spirit.

But some situations aren't so black and white. Every day each of us has to make choices about things that aren't blatantly sinful. What about selling ourselves short in a business meeting, not volunteering to do something we're able to do, not taking a risk because there's a chance we'll fail, not stepping out and trying something difficult that would move us closer to the fulfillment of a dream? That too might be sinful.

The point is this: *As we learn to listen to God's whispers, we have far better odds of knowing what's sinful and what isn't, and discovering our destiny.* For the Lord is faithful, and His advice is true, just as the prophet wrote: "Whether you turn to the right or to the left, your ears will hear a voice behind you, saying, 'This is the way; walk in it'" (Isaiah 30:21).

About This Book — and You

When we started thinking about the subject and outline of this book, we were in the midst of shifting jobs, starting a company, and preparing our older children to leave home. We didn't know exactly what was going to happen, and in fact, what happened was different from many of our expectations.

We don't know what will happen to you as a result of reading this book, but there are many possibilities. You may decide to change jobs. You may decide to take a risk and step out on a dream that's been silently trolling the waters of your mind for years. You may recognize that you have settled for mediocrity in some area of your life and begin to dream of living on a higher plane. You may decide to help someone you love pursue a lifelong dream. You may find new courage to start or invent something that will change history. You may realize that you're doing exactly what you were created to do and the restlessness within you is caused by something else. You may make small changes that cause you to feel less restless. You may begin to feel more "at home" with God and therefore yourself.

There is no limit to what could come out of your reading, because God knows no limits.

This book is not just for men and women who want to discover their own destiny — although this is critically important. It's in discovering our own destiny that we allow God to bring out the best in us, and this leads us to bring out the best in others (not *our* best for them, but God's best).

This book is for parents who care about helping their children become what they were created to be. It's for husbands and wives—and friends—who are committed to the other's best. It's for teachers who care about their students and employers who care about their employees. It is, in short, for anyone who believes that God has uniquely created each individual for a specific purpose and understands that when that purpose is discovered, a person can more effectively do His will and experience fullness of life while here on earth.

We can't promise that each person who reads this book will make a life-changing discovery. Much of that depends on you and your relationship and communication with God. We can promise you, though, that the potential is there—for new insights, new doors to open, new paths to take, new dreams to dream—because God is there, ready, waiting, and more interested than you are that you discover why He made you.

We'd like to suggest that you move through the book slowly, perhaps one chapter per sitting, and read with a pen and small notebook or journal nearby. That way when you come to Growth Ops, you can record your responses all in one place so that they're easily accessible to refer to on your journey.

This book is by both of us, Bill and Kathy. Sometimes you'll read I, Bill, sometimes I, Kathy. Sometimes "we" means Bill and Kathy and sometimes "we" means all of us—children of God, human beings. Who wrote what isn't that important because we're all in this together—both of us and all of you—trying to discover and live out the destiny for which we were created.

May he give you the desire of your heart
and make all your plans succeed. (Psalm 20:4)

Pulling Stakes and Jumping Fences

If we did all we are capable of doing, we would literally astonish ourselves.

THOMAS A. EDISON

What is impossible with men is possible with God.

JESUS CHRIST, LUKE 18:27

I **tried to appear brave,** but I was shaking in my Keds as we stood within five feet of a six-ton elephant tethered just outside the circus tent. I had seen elephants at the zoo before, behind iron bars, but this was different. My second-grade mind didn't understand the laws of physics, but somehow I knew that the short red-and-white stake ol' Jumbo was chained to was no match for his brawn. I can still see him in my mind, rocking back and forth and tugging against the stake, but never pulling it up.

My dad took my hand and told me I didn't need to be afraid. Then he asked, "Billy, do you know why such a little stake can hold a big elephant? When the big elephant was little, he was chained to a stake just like that baby." He pointed to a baby elephant nearby who seemed to be pulling with more determination than the big guy and explained how the stake was big enough to hold him at that age. "He pulled against it, over and over again, but it wouldn't budge. Then one day he gave up. He decided it was no use; he was just not strong enough. And an elephant never forgets."

I've often thought about that elephant. I find it fascinating that only one thing limits that six-ton elephant from getting where he wants to go—and it's not a two-foot stake. It's a thought.

That elephant reminds me a lot of myself sometimes. I live within limits that come nowhere close to my full potential. Some are self-imposed—I tried, failed, and decided I'd avoid that in the future—and some I've allowed other people to impose on me. More than a few people have tried to tie me down by saying, "You can't do that!" or "I can't see you in that role." And I'm sad to confess, some of those people succeeded. Whether my limits are self-imposed or people-imposed, I have to realize that they make a difference in how I see myself.

In order for each of us to move toward becoming the person God created us to be and fulfill the purpose He created us to fulfill, we must pull some stakes and refuse to let limitations define us.

I'm not what people think I am. I'm not what I think I am. I'm not even what I think others think I am. I am who Christ says I am.

Don't get me wrong. I'm not saying we don't have limitations to our potential. If I sat down at Kathy's piano, I would demonstrate beyond a shadow of a doubt that I have very limited potential to become the next Van Cliburn. I am saying that many of our limitations are manmade or self-made—small stakes that needlessly hold us back, just like the one that curbed the elephant. If we accept these restraints that dictate what we can't do or can't be, then we will only know those things that are impossible with man, and never know what is possible with God.

What If?

Just imagine what our lives would be like if visionaries had refused to pull stakes and jump fences. Here are a few ways people have tried to stake down the human race to what they considered possible with human beings.

• •

Knife and pain are two words in surgery that must forever be associated in the consciousness of the patient. To this compulsory combination we shall have to adjust ourselves.

—DR. ALFRED VELPEAU, 19TH CENTURY PHYSICIAN

Thank you, Drs. William Morton, Horace Wells, and Crawford Long, for pioneering the use of anesthesia in surgery in the 1840s.

• •

The demonstration that no possible combination of known substances, known forms of machinery, and known forms of force can be united in a practical machine by which man shall fly long distances through the air, seems to the writer as complete as it is possible for the demonstration of any physical fact to be.

SIMON NEWCOMB, CANADIAN-BORN ASTRONOMER

Thank you, Wilbur and Orville Wright, for being bored with bicycles and pursuing your dream to fly.

• •

The advancement of the arts from year to year taxes our credulity and seems to presage the arrival of that period when further improvement must end.

—HENRY L. ELLSWORTH, U.S. COMMISSIONER OF PATENTS, 1844

Thank you, Elisha Otis, for the elevator (1852), Joseph Lister for antiseptic surgery (1865), Alexander Graham Bell for the telephone (1876), Carl Benz for the automobile engine (1879), W. H. Carrier for air conditioning (1911), Sir Alexander Fleming for penicillin (1928), and of course, Thomas Edison for the phonograph (1877), the light bulb (1879), and motion pictures (1893).

Knock Yourself Out

I hung up the phone, rocked back in my chair, and pondered the words I had just heard. One of our consultants wrapped up her conversation with me by saying, "Knock yourself out!" Her admonition took me a little by surprise. Usually I hear (and say myself, as well), "Take it easy!" As I thought about it, her phrase was far more biblical,

• •

Life is like a ten-speed bike. Most of us have gears we never use.

—CHARLES SCHULTZ

although not in the sense that we should beat ourselves up or work ourselves to death. What she was telling me was to astonish myself with my performance. And why shouldn't I? After all, I have a great and mighty, all-powerful God. The way I figure it, if a few of us pushed our preconceived limits more often, resting in God's power, we might just push our brain power closer to the potential God invested in us.

All of us know instinctively that we were created for something more than we experience on a daily basis. The dreams we had when we were young of possessing magical powers had some basis in God's reality. We long to experience more than we do, to be more than we are, to accomplish more than we "can." Something within calls us to a larger, better reality than we can grasp—one

20

not constrained by time, space, and resources. With our feet firmly planted in the earthly actuality of the visible world, dreaming stretches us to weigh spiritual possibilities beyond our five senses.

• •

Everyone knows that on any given day there are energies slumbering in him which the incitements of the day do not call forth. . . . Compared with what we ought to be, we are only half awake. Our fires are damped, our drafts are checked. We are making use of only a small part of our possible mental and physical resources. . . . Stating the thing broadly, the human individual thus lives far within his limits; he possesses powers of various sorts he habitually fails to use.

—WILLIAM JAMES, "ENERGIES OF MEN," *MEMORIES AND STUDIES* (1917)

An Astounding Promise

It's depressing enough to think about the untapped potential of the human race in general, but if we consider unrealized spiritual resources as well, the situation becomes even more tragic. Just before Jesus returned to heaven, He made an astounding promise to His disciples: "I tell you

What areas in your life are you putting a limit on God because you've put a limit on yourself?

the truth, anyone who has faith in me will do what I have been doing. He will do even greater things than these, because I am going to the Father" (John 14:12).

What did Jesus mean by this? Was He talking about greater quality (bigger, more dramatic things) or greater quantity (more of them)? Was He talking about things in the realm of the miraculous and unbelievable, or the daily and mundane? Whatever this verse means, it defies reasonable explanation. What is promised here is *not* reasonable—like so many of Jesus' promises. When we allow this verse to seep into our thinking, it's guaranteed to move us beyond our predictable, manageable, reasonable comfort zone into an unpredictable, unmanageable, and unreasonable zone. We'll be living so far beyond our human capabilities that we'll be required to live by faith for sheer survival. That's our destiny!

> God gives us always strength enough, and sense enough, for everything he wants us to do.
>
> —JOHN RUSKIN,
> BRITISH WRITER AND ART CRITIC

A Remarkable Power

Jesus has ventured a great deal in each of us—so much, in fact, that the apostle Paul is at a loss for words as he describes the power God invests in us. "Now to Him who is able to do exceeding abundantly beyond all that we ask or think, according to the power that works within us, to Him be the glory" (Ephesians 3:20, NASB).

"Exceeding abundantly"! These are lavish superlatives overflowing with significance. The reach of our small requests and puny imaginations cannot begin to embrace the competence God has bestowed upon us. And this being the case, it stands to reason that the wildest, most impossible dreams that flit through our heads fall within the realm of feasibility. (Only God's purpose and His character limit the possibilities.)

A Sad Fact

Dreaming what is possible for God, however, often seems like risky business and, unfortunately, playing it safe is many times the preferred and seemingly prudent course of action. Listening to some Christian leaders, we might well wonder just what we need faith for. They suggest that if we simply follow their principles, go by their rules, stay within their well-drawn lines, then everything will go right. They argue for a sort of "warning track" Christianity that advocates avoiding risk, playing it safe, coloring inside the lines.

Our Border collie puppy, Kit, has the same tendency to play it safe. We wanted her to be able to run free when we weren't around, but we didn't want her wandering into the street, so we installed an invisible electric fence around the perimeter of our lot. Kit wears a special collar that will give her a slight shock if she steps too close to her "fence." One shock was enough for her to know she didn't want to get near the edge again. So, even though she has a lot more yard to roam in, she plays in the center, far within her boundaries.

> He that is overcautious will accomplish little.
>
> —JOHANN VON SCHILLER, GERMAN POET

The sad truth is that most of us, like our overcautious puppy, live far within our limits. But when did safety become the ultimate objective of the Christian life? Why has it become a virtue to waste our potential?

> The poor man is not he who is without a cent, but he who is without a dream.
>
> —HARRY KEMP

Recently, an old friend called us to catch up on things. We mentioned that our twenty-two-year-old son John was going to Hollywood for an internship with a company that does computerized special effects for film and television. This opportunity is a dream come true for John. Interestingly, our friend couldn't believe we would "let" our "child" live in such a dangerous, excessive place. The implication was that we must be irresponsible and permissive parents. We are neither. When you want to raise your children to be strong in their faith, to use the gifts and talents God has given them to make an impact on our culture for Him, you have to be willing to let them take risks.

The truth of the matter is that God made the whole world, and there is no place where He is not present. Geography and circumstances have little to do with real security when placed against the backdrop of the purpose of God. No matter what earthly dangers exist, the safest place to be is following Christ—wherever He leads. No matter how safe and secure some places and situations seem, we're on shaky ground if it is not God's desire for us to be there.

If God meant for us to live inside an invisible fence, why did He place some of His choicest servants in prison, a lions' den, a human-size furnace, a shipwrecked boat? Why did He send Paul to Rome or Jonah to Nineveh or Esther to the palace in Persia? Because they had purposes to fulfill—destinies—and God meant for them to discover the unlimited nature of His power and love, which aren't, by the way, discovered when we retreat to the safety zone. The world is here. It's not safe. But we have to deal with it. If we do so with faith—which starts with confidence in God's love for us—we'll discover a potential for impact. We can make a *big* impact in "small" places (which aren't really small at all), like raising our kids to be confident in who they are and what they believe even when they go against the grain of culture. And we can make a big impact in big places—work, government, schools.

Here's the bottom line: *If God is everywhere and in everything, He is calling for us to follow Him back to the street to redeem a world caught in the vise grip of death. If we stay on the porch, where it's supposedly safe, we'll not only miss our destiny, but the roof may collapse—and we'll deserve it!*

> Life is either a daring adventure or nothing.
>
> —HELEN KELLER

The Greatest Threat

> What would life be if we had no courage to attempt anything?
>
> —VINCENT VAN GOGH

In 1978 we had the privilege of attending a series of lectures by Christian philosopher Dr. Francis Schaeffer. He predicted that the greatest threat to the cause of Jesus Christ as we approached the end of the twentieth century would be if the United States became a nation filled with Christians whose goal in life is personal peace (or safety) and prosperity. Were he still alive, he could watch his prediction coming to pass. When safety and prosperity become our passions, we can be sure we've abandoned the pursuit of our God-given destiny in favor of a substandard life. If we were honest, we'd have to admit that this attitude is one of pure and simple fear. We don't take risks, we don't dream about doing great things because we're afraid that if we don't protect ourselves and our stuff, we'll lose what's ours — or what we *think* is ours. Ironically, we are never more vulnerable than when we are playing it safe.

● ●

You can live on bland food so as to avoid an ulcer; drink no tea or coffee or other stimulants, in the name of health; go to bed early and stay away from night life; avoid all controversial subjects so as never to give offense; mind your own business and avoid involvement in other people's problems; spend money only on necessities and save all you can. You can still break your neck in the bathtub, and it will serve you right.

—Eileen Guder, contemporary American Author

When we refuse to dream beyond our own greeds to the world's great needs, what we're really thinking is that *this is all there is — what I see is what I get*. Period. Case closed.

But beware. This kind of thinking has serious spiritual implications. To accept things "as is," to acquiesce and say "this is just the way things are," to embrace the status quo as the only possibility, is to accept Satan's destructive presence in the world as the final reality and refuse to believe in God's power and passion to redeem and fulfill His creation.

But what really happens, according to God's "economy," is that when we operate like that, our borders shrink, our boundaries get smaller and smaller, and we get farther and farther away from God — not risk. In other words, we fence ourselves off with a false sense of security and tether ourselves to a stake that keeps us from everyone, including God. Our love for Christ will grow cold, our passion

GrowthOp

Take a piece of paper and list your stakes and fences. How are you like the elephant and the collie?

Have you told yourself lately or heard someone tell you, "You can't do that!"? Who really says you can't? God? Someone else? Yourself? Is it really true according to God's Word?

damp. After all, what do we need Him for if we have everything buttoned down tight in our little world?

If we reach out, though, and tear down the fences and pull up the stakes with God's help at hand and His purpose in mind, we'll find everything about us changing. Our senses will be sharpened, and our love for Christ ignited.

• •

So do not fear, for I am with you;
  do not be dismayed, for I am your God.
I will strengthen you and help you;
  I will uphold you with my righteous right hand.
    (Isaiah 41:10)

26

Set Apart—
On Purpose

*Here is the test to find
whether your mission on earth
is finished: If you're alive, it isn't.*

RICHARD BACH, AMERICAN AUTHOR

Why do I exist? Where do I fit in? What do I have to offer this world? What is my purpose? Do I have a destiny? Deep within every human being is a longing to know the reason for his or her existence. We know we have been created by God to be somebody and to do something significant. Yet, for all of us who search and ask these questions, few find satisfying answers. We lose heart because we don't go to the Source of meaning and purpose, God Himself.

• •

Life's but a walking shadow, a poor player
That struts and frets his hour upon the stage,
And then is heard no more; it is a tale
Told by an idiot full of sound and fury,
Signifying nothing.

—WILLIAM SHAKESPEARE

Perhaps if we're honest, we'd confess that when we're alone with our thoughts, we think Shakespeare was right. Often, life does not make sense. It carries us along in a tide of mindless circumstances we can't imagine how to escape from, much less make any sense of. We question whether or not life really has meaning and purpose. It seems like those of us who profess to know God, of all people, should have a clearer picture of what He wants us to do with our lives. After all, He is our Designer. But, in reality, many Christians feel that finding God's will is like the quest for the Holy Grail: You search all your life for the elusive assurance that you are where you're supposed to be—in the "center" of God's will—and all the while you're not really sure that it can be found, or sometimes if it even exists in the first place.

Very few people are confident they have found God's will, and most, it seems, are wandering through life with the vague notion that there must be something more to life. They wish they were doing something else—sometimes anything else—so they could experience fulfillment and feel significant as human beings. Others feel that life is something merely to be endured until we get to heaven—and it's only natural to feel unfulfilled this side of heaven's gates. Yet, if we believe God created us for a purpose, how can we shelve that purpose until some future date?

> It's never too late to be what you could have been.
>
> —GEORGE ELIOT, ENGLISH NOVELIST

If we truly desire to know our destiny, the purpose for which we were created, there is only one place to turn in our search—to the Creator, the Author of meaning and purpose.

In fact, that Author has emphatically encouraged us to follow Him: "My sheep listen to my voice; I know them, and they follow me" (John 10:27); and "Whoever serves me must follow me; and where I am, my servant also will be" (12:26).

If Jesus calls us to follow, then the big question is: *Where is He leading?*

Taking God at His Word

The notion of God having a specific plan for our lives is not a myth. As we can see from His Word, God created people individually and gave them specific tasks to accomplish. For example, in Genesis 2:15, He told Adam to work and take care of the garden. God made him, then put him to work doing what he was made for. The fact is, no matter how far and wide we search, we'll never find the ultimate fulfillment and feeling of significance we long for apart from knowing the infinite God who designed us and what He designed us for.

> You can't make proper use of a thing unless you know what it was made for, whether it is a safety pin or a sailboat.
>
> —ELISABETH ELLIOT, AMERICAN AUTHOR

The good news is, God is not hiding His purpose for us. His will is not buried in some faraway place that requires a lifelong quest to discover. He is not playing hide-and-seek with our destiny. Quite the contrary: God is much more interested in our discovering our destiny and doing His will than we are. Jesus, in His Sermon on the Mount, made it clear how accessible He is: "Ask and it will be given to you; seek and you will find; knock and the door will be opened to you. For everyone who asks receives; he who seeks finds; and to him who knocks, the door will be opened" (Matthew 7:7-8).

Perhaps the reason we have so much trouble finding out why we're here and what we're supposed to be doing is because we don't knock. Or maybe we're knocking at the wrong doors or refusing to go through the doors that are opened. Maybe we're asking the wrong people or not listening to the answers. Whatever the reason, it's important that we understand that *God's will is not something we find someplace "out there"; it starts right where we are.*

• •

Some things have to be believed to be seen.

—LYNN YEAKEL, 1994 CANDIDATE U.S. SENATE

"For I know the plans I have for you,"
    declares the LORD,
"plans to prosper you and not to harm you,
    plans to give you hope and a future."

—JEREMIAH 29:11

This verse ought to give us a great deal of hope and comfort, as well as a sense of anticipation. But as many times as we've heard it, perplexingly, many of us simply can't figure out the plans God has for us. We balk at making decisions that affect our future. We become immobilized when we can't seem to discern God's voice. We second-guess our decisions when things don't go as expected.

There's a reason for this, and it's a reason we don't like to admit. Simply put, we have not developed an intimate relationship with God, a deep relationship that makes His voice familiar enough to recognize above the cacophony of voices—from within and without—calling out instructions and plans for us.

Everyone seems to have a plan for our lives. Tom's father and grandfather were attorneys, so he thinks, *I'm expected to follow in their footsteps.* Sally would rather be home with her children, but she thinks, *My parents paid for my education, and they expect me to be "gainfully employed."* The only role models Brad sees really serving God are his pastors, so he thinks, *I should quit my job and go to seminary.* Susan knows she's a very good nurse and loves her work, but her friends say she's an inferior mother because she works outside the home. They tell her, "You should give up nursing for your family."

There Is a Plan

If you have breath you have purpose. If you have a purpose, you have a destiny. Destiny is not something reserved for the famous or fabulously gifted. Every single human being has been specifically designed

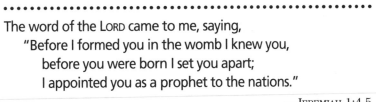

The word of the LORD came to me, saying,
  "Before I formed you in the womb I knew you,
    before you were born I set you apart;
    I appointed you as a prophet to the nations."

—JEREMIAH 1:4-5

for his or her appearance in history, and God did the designing.

Whether you are a college student with your life ahead of you, a business person who is looking for more, or someone who is fearful of what retirement holds (or doesn't hold), the desire to escape the monotony of routine existence is no abrogation. God has placed the need for purpose in each of our hearts. That purpose is not something we can define ourselves. Contrary to the idea that we can become anything we want to be, we are not a blank slate to be written on, a lump of clay to be molded by outside, often conflicting forces. We come into this world predesigned with God-given, specific abilities He has bestowed upon us to accomplish His purposes.

> Next to the Incarnation, I know of no more staggering truth
> than that a sovereign God has ordained my participation.
>
> —ELISABETH ELLIOT

Men and Women of Destiny

Our job is to discern how we can best accomplish God's purpose. We should learn all we can from the resources God has given us—parents, friends, spouse, boss, pastor, books, wisdom of the ages. But ultimately, we must evaluate every voice, internal or external, by God's Word to see if it belongs to Him.

Using the above resources as a starting point, think about the resources you have. What talks have you had lately about your future? What has your own inner voice been telling you? Then make a list of five or six specific pieces of information. Reread them carefully. The ultimate question is: Do they belong to God?

Before we examine the tree, we need to describe the forest—the big picture. We are emphasizing the purpose for which God has set us apart in this chapter, and God has made His general purposes for our lives very clear in the pages of the Old and New Testaments. There we find three main aspects of His will.

1. God desires that we know Him in a personal and intimate way. The God of the Bible is not some detached deity who created the world and then withdrew His presence. He is a person, and as such He desires a personal relationship, a deep intimacy, a wonderful love relationship, between creature and Creator.

God created us for intimacy with Himself and placed a corresponding longing for intimacy within us.

> You have made us for Yourself, O God,
> and the heart of man is restless until it
> finds rest in You.
>
> —SAINT AUGUSTINE

God has promised: Those who seek Him with all their heart will find Him and know Him.

The apostle Paul speaks of this longing to know God in his letter to the Philippians: "I consider everything a loss compared to the surpassing greatness of knowing Christ Jesus my Lord, for whose sake I have lost all things. . . . I want to know Christ" (Philippians 3:8,10).

• •

"You will call upon me and come and pray to me,
    and I will listen to you.
You will seek me and find me
    when you seek me with all your heart."

—JEREMIAH 29:12-13

It is truly an amazing idea to ponder: *the Creator of the universe wants a personal relationship with us.*

2. God desires that we submit to His authority and be conformed to His image. Genesis 1:27 tells us that man was created in the image of God. When the human race rebelled against God's authority, sin marred the image of God in every human being. But He loves us too much to leave us in that condition. He is reshaping our character to be like that of Christ.

> *We know that in all things God works for the good of those who love him, who have been called according to his purpose. For those God foreknew he also predestined to be conformed to the likeness of his Son, that he might be the firstborn among many brothers. (Romans 8:28-29)*

Now, as we grow in our knowledge of God, His image is being restored in us. He is gradually, incrementally accomplishing this aspect of His will. "But we all, with unveiled face beholding as in a mirror the glory of the Lord, are being transformed into the same image from glory to glory, just as from the Lord, the Spirit" (2 Corinthians 3:18, NASB).

As we grow, we recognize more and more of Christ's character being formed in us, and we realize that God deserves to occupy the place in our hearts that He occupies in the universe—Lord of all. As our relationship with God grows deeper, more and more of our desire to run our own lives apart from Him is crowded out and replaced by a glad submission to His authority in our lives. We're not talking about becoming will-less. We're talking about getting smart about life. The more we know God, the more stupid it seems to resist His will—not because He's bigger and stronger than we are, but because He is the source of joy.

• •

You have made known to me the path of life;
  you will fill me with joy in your presence,
  with eternal pleasures at your right hand.

—PSALM 16:11

We like the way C. S. Lewis explains how God works in us.

Imagine yourself as a living house. God comes in to rebuild that house. At first, perhaps, you can understand what He is doing. He is getting the drains right and stopping the leaks in the roof and so on: you knew that those jobs needed doing and so you are not surprised. But presently He starts knocking the house about in a way that hurts abominably and does not seem to make sense. What on earth is He up to? The explanation is that He is building quite a different house from the one you thought of—throwing out a new wing here, putting on an extra floor there, running up towers, making courtyards. You thought you were going to be made into a decent little cottage: but He is building a palace. He intends to come and live in it Himself.[1]

3. God wants us to be involved in His work. He has called us to do much more than hang out on planet earth. We're here on a mission. He has called us to reclaim territory previously held by His enemy

Satan since the Garden of Eden episode, to be involved in the redemption of all of His creation.

All this is from God, who reconciled us to himself through Christ and gave us the ministry of reconciliation: that God was reconciling the world to himself in Christ, not counting men's sins against them. And he has committed to us the message of reconciliation. We are therefore Christ's ambassadors, as though God were making his appeal through us. We implore you on Christ's behalf: Be reconciled to God. (2 Corinthians 5:18-20)

But our mission involves much more than reconciliation. Even before sin entered the picture, Adam and Eve were busy doing God's work, developing His creation. He told them, "Be fruitful and increase in number; fill the earth and subdue it. Rule over the fish of the sea and the birds of the air and over every living creature that moves on the ground" (Genesis 1:28).

The human race was placed here to colonize the planet in God's name—to develop its resources,

Which of the following best describes you?

1. I love my work. I'm cooking on all four burners. But sometimes I wonder exactly what I'm cooking.
2. I feel like I'm making meat loaf, when I want to be running a four-star restaurant. That is, I feel like I have untapped talent and potential I don't have an opportunity to express.
3. I know what I've always wanted to do, and I'm going to figure out a way to do it.
4. I feel like a microwave oven that spends its days trying to be a toaster oven. My life just ain't happening.

Then, take your answer—and your question—to God. When I'm feeling like I don't know my own mind, is it God's mind I'm not getting acquainted with? When things aren't happening, have I considered the possibility that I'm using willpower when I should be submitting to His will? When I'm confused about what I should be doing, do I ask God?

advance culture, evolve technology, tame the wilds, and provide for human need. It's hard to imagine where the human race would be today if it were unthrottled by sin, selfishness, and ignorance.

Unfortunately, some people latch onto the idea of knowing God and stop right there. They spend so much of their time preoccupied with their personal growth and spiritual development that they miss God's mission for their lives. The idea is to "do" as well as "be." These two aspects of the Christian life are inseparable.

What I am to *be* is apparent.

What I am to *do* is the rub.

How, you may be wondering, *do I know my mission? What is God's specific work and will for me?* If God is really God, then knowing His will, finding out for what purpose we've been set apart, discovering our destiny, is an awfully high priority. Spending time on anything else will leave us frustrated and empty. On the other hand, spending time with God, discovering our mission, will fill us up, even as we encounter frustrations and obstacles along the way.

> Firmness of purpose is one of the most necessary sinews of character, and one of the best instruments of success. Without it genius wastes its efforts in a maze of inconsistencies.
>
> —LORD CHESTERFIELD,
> ENGLISH STATESMAN

One Man Who Discovered His Destiny

The Bible is full of fascinating accounts of how God has revealed His will to men and women since the beginning of time. One person, however, stands out as a paradigm, or model, for our consideration. He was an ordinary man who had an undeniable passion and an extraordinary dream in his heart. This dreamer was Nehemiah. We can learn a lot from him, but two things in particular: We can observe how God led, and how Nehemiah listened and discovered what God wanted him to do. And we can examine and learn from the way Nehemiah, once he understood his mission, pursued his destiny and fulfilled God's plan.

Maybe you're thinking, *Oh, great, what can I—a banker, teacher, manager, doctor, plumber, secretary, family manager, whatever—learn from some ancient Bible character? What could he possibly know about the world I live in and the pressures I face every day? His story may work well on a flannelboard, but it doesn't work for me.*

If this describes how you're feeling, please don't stop reading. Give God's Word a chance. We'll admit, Nehemiah's world was vastly different from ours, but the God who led Nehemiah to discover his destiny is the same God who leads us today. We think He leads us in a very similar way. Understanding the principles of His guidance will help you get closer to discovering your destiny than you've ever been before.

In fact, these principles will head you right to the answer itself.

3

Ancient Dream — Modern Paradigm

To sit alone in the lamplight
with a book spread out before you,
and hold intimate converse
with men of unseen generations —
such is a pleasure beyond compare.

YOSHIDA KENKO

These things happened to them
as an example, and they were
written for our instruction.

THE APOSTLE PAUL, 1 CORINTHIANS 10:11, NASB

Century after century, generation after generation, people and circumstances change. But as the old saying goes, "The more things change, the more they stay the same." No matter the moment in history, men and women have always dreamed dreams.

Nehemiah was a dreamer. According to Webster, a dreamer is someone who has ideas or schemes that are considered impractical. But it's difficult to discern God's purpose for us without dreaming. We all need to become dreamers. Nehemiah was one of the most sensible leaders in the Old Testament, but his grand public-works project to restore the walls of Jerusalem was anything but practical. At first glance, his idea seemed downright ridiculous. In actuality, it was an idea that only a true man of faith could have dared to entertain. It was a dream that only a person of wisdom could have accomplished.

When God placed this dream in Nehemiah's heart, the Jews had been a part of Babylon and then Persian life for more than a century and a half, ever since Nebuchadnezzar captured Jerusalem and began deporting Jewish citizens in 605 B.C. From the very beginning of this captivity, Israelites were forced by their captors into the service of the king, not merely as laborers, but as key advisors and officials in the kingdom as well. Men like Daniel and women like Esther found themselves in places of great influence in ancient Near Eastern affairs. Nehemiah also became one of these influential individuals. Though he was a Jew, he was raised in Persia, a pagan culture. Yet his faith in God was strong and unvarnished by exposure to an ungodly environment.

Nehemiah served faithfully in the palace of King Artexerxes. Over the years he had risen to perhaps the most trusted position in the empire—cupbearer to the king. The life expectancy of an ancient Near Eastern monarch was short, to say the least. The cupbearer was the equivalent of today's top secret service agent who is willing to step in front of a bullet to save the president's life. In Nehemiah's day, the cupbearer put his life on the line daily by tasting every dish and sampling every drink that was set before the king to ensure that it had not been poisoned. Because of their close relationship and the risks he willingly accepted for the sake of the king, the cupbearer often became the king's chief advisor.

Some ninety years before Nehemiah's story begins, the Persians defeated the Babylonians, and King Cyrus decided to allow the Jews to begin their return to Palestine. During that time, some fifty thousand Jews had returned to their homeland. But many others, entrenched in Persian life, remained behind.

It must have been hard for Nehemiah to watch his friends, relatives, and countrymen return to the land of his heart. If you've ever longed to be somewhere other than where you were, for whatever reason, you know how Nehemiah must have felt.

Whatever Nehemiah's reasons for staying in Persia, we do know two important facts: First, his failure to return with the faithful to Jerusalem is not a negative commentary on his devotion to God. He knew he could serve the one and only God right where he was. Susa, however, was no friendly environment for the cultivation of faith. The winter capital of Persia, Susa was the seat of wealth and power. The beautiful people gathered there to amuse themselves and deaden the pain of an empty existence. All of the perversions, excesses, and human cruelty that unlimited prosperity and unchecked power produce were present. In that environment, devoid of spiritual encouragement, Nehemiah not only survived, but flourished. Unlike so many who are taken captive by temptation, he was challenging the Enemy's influence, not only on his heart, but on those around him. He was a man of God in every sense.

Second, Nehemiah had no envy or bitterness toward those who got to return or those who may have made him stay. The quality of Nehemiah's work and loyalty to King Artexerxes, a boss who, by the way, did not share Nehemiah's values, was exemplary in every way. Nehemiah shows us clearly that the conflict between serving God and pursuing excellence in your work is not a foregone conclusion.

The Jews had been exiled into captivity because of their refusal to place the one true God above foreign idols. They were warned and

· ·

Excellence is not a matter of chance, it's a matter of choice.

41

warned, but they persisted. God's message, given through His prophets, was simple: Shape up or I will ship you out. Unfortunately, like most of us, they had to learn the hard way. But God also promised that when they repented and turned back to Him in faithfulness, He would let them return to their homeland and restore Jerusalem. Seventy years earlier, Zerubbabel had returned and led the rebuilding of God's temple. Thirteen years earlier, Ezra had returned to rebuild the people spiritually. Yet, things weren't going as smoothly as they might.

Like many dreams, Nehemiah's story began with some bad news. On a crisp winter evening in the month of Kislev in 445 B.C. (the precise time would have been December of 445, during the twentieth year of the reign of King Artexerxes, who ruled Persia from 464 to 425), weary travelers brought news from Jerusalem that would rock his world.

> *In the month of Kislev in the twentieth year, while I was in the citadel of Susa, Hanani, one of my brothers, came from Judah with some other men, and I questioned them about the Jewish remnant that survived the exile, and also about Jerusalem.*
>
> *They said to me, "Those who survived the exile and are back in the province are in great trouble and disgrace. The wall of Jerusalem is broken down, and its gates have been burned with fire." (Nehemiah 1:1-3)*

Nehemiah's life was forever changed by this simple bit of information that arrived via camel all the way from Jerusalem. Had there been *Headline News* in 445 B.C., here's how we might have heard the story.

FROM SUSA, PERSIA — THIS WORD JUST IN FROM THE PALACE. EMISSARIES ARRIVED TODAY FROM JERUSALEM BRINGING WORD OF THE STATE OF THE WESTERN BOUNDARIES OF THE EMPIRE. AFTER THEIR ARDUOUS JOURNEY, THE EMISSARIES WERE NOTICEABLY UPSET

AND IMMEDIATELY SOUGHT AN APPOINTMENT WITH THE
KING. A SOURCE CLOSE TO THE GROUP REVEALED THAT
THEY WISHED TO CONFRONT THE KING REGARDING HIS
EDICT TO CEASE REBUILDING THE CAPITAL CITY OF THE
JEWS. APPARENTLY THE KING'S OFFICIALS HAD NOT
ONLY HALTED CONSTRUCTION, BUT HAD ORDERED THE
GATES BURNED, BRINGING FURTHER RUIN AND MAKING
RECONSTRUCTION VIRTUALLY IMPOSSIBLE.

THIS WAS VERY BAD NEWS FOR THE JEWS, WHO
HAVE BEEN IMMIGRATING TO THEIR HOMELAND NOW FOR
OVER NINETY YEARS. ONE OF THE EMISSARIES, HANANI,
IS THE BROTHER OF NEHEMIAH, THE KING'S CUPBEARER.
REPORTEDLY, HANANI HOPED FOR A QUICK AUDIENCE
WITH THE KING BECAUSE OF HIS BROTHER'S
CONNECTIONS. NEHEMIAH, ONE OF THE KING'S MOST
TRUSTED SERVANTS, WAS UNAVAILABLE FOR COMMENT.

THE ARMY CHIEF OF STAFF, HOWEVER, ISSUED THIS
STATEMENT: "THE KING HAS RECEIVED INTELLIGENCE
INDICATING THAT THE JEWS PLAN TO REVOLT AS SOON
AS JERUSALEM IS DEFENSIBLE AGAIN. THIS WAS A
PREEMPTIVE STRIKE. WE WISH TO REMOVE THE THREAT
BEFORE IT'S CARRIED OUT. ACCORDING TO THE PRESS
COORDINATOR, THE CONSENSUS AT THE PALACE IS THAT
'THE JEWS HAVE SHOWN A CONSISTENT TRACK RECORD
OF POLITICAL VOLATILITY AND CANNOT BE TRUSTED
WITH SELF-RULE.'"

Hanani brought sad news for the faithful Jews still in Persia. As long as Jerusalem lay in ruins, the Jews would never be secure enough to live there (today this would be tantamount to living in a house without locks), Jerusalem would remain uninhabited, and the city where God had caused His name to dwell would remain in ruins. No doubt many faithful Jews in Persia heard the news and were saddened, feeling even more keenly the pain of their separation from their countrymen. Some sighed. Some wept. Some prayed. Nehemiah was deeply distressed. His response is recorded in his memoirs.

When I heard these things, I sat down and wept. For some days I mourned and fasted and prayed before the God of heaven. Then I said:

"O LORD, God of heaven, the great and awesome God, who keeps his covenant of love with those who love him and obey his commands, let your ear be attentive and your eyes open to hear the prayer your servant is praying before you day and night for your servants, the people of Israel." (Nehemiah 1:4-6)

Paradigm for a Dreamer

According to the dictionary, a paradigm is an outstandingly clear or typical example. We all know the outcome of Nehemiah's story. It's history. In brief: He heard the bad news; he responded passionately; he prayed. With God's help, he turned his passionate response into a dream. He kept on track: He prepared himself; he continued praying; he planned. He did all this during the time it took for his dream to begin, and while his dream was being fulfilled.

Over the course of the rest of this book, as we look at our own dreams and the steps needed to make them become reality, we will return to Nehemiah and his dream of rebuilding the walls of Jerusalem. Part of the reason Nehemiah's story is such a wonderful paradigm is that it charts each of the steps, along with the possible pitfalls, we go through as our dreams become reality. But there's another reason Nehemiah's story works so well as a paradigm for modern times. It's not about process. It's about content.

We are not, of course, called to rebuild the walls of Jerusalem literally. But, whatever we are called to do, if it is a dream from God, it will bear some resemblance to rebuilding Jerusalem's walls; that is, it will be something that furthers God's purpose on this earth. It will, in some way, large or small, affect the lives of God's people for the better. A dream to get married and raise our children to fulfill their God-given purpose, often in the face of critics and temptations to secularism, is like a dream to rebuild the walls of Jerusalem, as is a dream to begin a new business or start a new career or earn a college degree in mid-life, as long as it is done for the right reasons and has the greater glory of God as its ultimate end. If Nehemiah had embarked upon his task so he could be crowned king of the city, well, we wouldn't be reading his story. Or we'd be reading an entirely different story.

When Nehemiah heard the news about Jerusalem, it sank like an arrow directly into his heart. He wept *and* mourned *and* prayed *and* fasted. He did that because God whispered into his ear. God created in Nehemiah's heart a deep concern for Jerusalem and its people.

When Nehemiah heard the news, he didn't react compulsively, rushing in to the king, demanding that things change. He didn't lash out at those responsible. And he didn't engage in self-pity, thinking, *What can I do, I'm eight hundred miles away?*

Growth Op

Have you ever heard news that made you lie awake nights or weep? That made you pound the table for emphasis as you thought, *Someone has got to do something about . . . ?* If you have, you know to some degree how Nehemiah felt. Begin a list of these "bad news" situations. They can be a clue to discovering your passion and implementing your dream.

Great minds have purposes, others have wishes. Little minds are tamed and subdued by misfortune; but great minds rise above them.

—Washington Irving

Nehemiah entered the door. He didn't stop in self-pity at the very threshold of the greatest adventure of his life. For a dreamer, despair over bad news isn't the signal to stop. It's the signal to cry out to God and to listen to the answer. It's a signal to keep on keeping on, because we might be on the very threshold of adventure.

We sit down at the door of God's purpose and enter a slow death through self-pity.

—Oswald Chambers

> ## Growth Op
>
> If you truly want to know God's will for your life, is your heart prepared to do His will—whatever it is? Be honest with yourself. What have you thought of doing but said you never would or never could in a million years? Could this be something God is calling you to do?

God will always reveal His will to one who is willing to do it.

—Hilys Jasper

It's interesting to note that Nehemiah had time, or at least he took time, a lot of time, to pray and listen. We who are accustomed to ten-minute lube jobs and one-hour photo processing would like to skip over this issue of praying and waiting and get on with our very important purpose-pursuing business. Truth to tell, most of us would like an on-the-spot, dramatic sign to lead us to our destiny. The tap of an angel on our shoulder in between appointments would work. Or maybe before we fall into bed we'd like to lay out a fleece as Gideon did. Even a word from the family pet would suffice. I mean, didn't Balaam's donkey speak to him? God could certainly do any of these things. But most of the time, He guides us in what seems to be very quiet, unrushed, natural ways—just as He did Nehemiah.

God still speaks to those who have time to listen.

If we want to learn to recognize God's whisper in our heart, then we have to be quiet and still long enough to listen.

Recently, Kathy was out of town and I was faced with filling in for two parents as cook, chauffeur, teacher, coach, and housekeeper. I had to confess to an insightful friend that my world has been so fast, cluttered, and noisy lately, that I wasn't sure I could hear God speak if He used a loudspeaker. It's precisely times like these—when one of us is traveling a lot, when we're working on deadlines for several projects, or when things are simply hectic—that we need to slow down and pay attention.

At times God whispers even to the busiest people. When our minds are scanning our experiential universe, like at night as we lie awake staring at the ceiling or in the morning when our thoughts churn while we run or work out, sometimes dreams serendipitously emerge. Or as we read the newspaper, a magazine, or the Bible, a quiet impression will come over us and we'll say, "I wish I could . . ." or "Someone has got to do something about . . ." The question here, of course, is how do we know when we're supposed to take the initiative and act on these stirrings?

We must learn to pay attention to promptings—quiet nudges in our heart, dreams within the depth our being. But it's also important that we learn to determine which ones are whispers from God and which ones are from indigestion or some other source. And it's also important that we know how to turn God-inspired dreams into reality. As we continue to work our way through Nehemiah's story, we'll find a model of how ordinary people who dream extraordinary dreams can see them become reality.

GrowthOp

Nehemiah thought he was set for life. He didn't know he had another great thing to accomplish until God told him. If God were to tell you right now that it would be possible for you to accomplish one great thing while you're here on earth, what would it be? (Not something you've already accomplished. Listen carefully. What is He calling you to do?)

• •

He who insists on seeing with perfect clearness before he decides never decides.

—HENRI-FREDERIC AMIEL, SWISS PHILOSOPHER

47

CHAPTER 4

2,500 Years Later, God Still Whispers

*Some men see things as they are
and say, "Why?" I dream things that
never were and say, "Why not?"*

GEORGE BERNARD SHAW

*"The simple truth is that if you had a
mere kernel of faith, a poppy seed, say,
you would tell this mountain, 'move!'
and it would move. There is nothing you
wouldn't be able to tackle."*

JESUS CHRIST, MATTHEW 17:20, *THE MESSAGE*

We believe that God still nudges, whispers, and gives us dreams. In fact, one of the ways God leads us is through our own desires and dreams, dreams we may have had from childhood, dreams we have relegated to the back burner or the back shelf of the closet because they seem irrelevant, impractical, impossible. Remember, things that are impossible on our own can sometimes be as much fun, and as creative and productive, as child's play when we put them in God's hands. Though it took her a while (like Nehemiah) to recognize His voice, that's what happened to Kathy nearly a decade ago. Little did she know her life was about to change forever.

It was a beautiful November morning in East Texas. The year was 1987. We were at an old, restored inn with ten couples for a retreat. Bill was the speaker, and his messages dealt with taking your dreams seriously and discovering God's will for your life. Trying to look like an attentive wife — hanging on my husband's every word — I was really thinking, *I don't have time to be here. Besides, I'm too busy taking care of three nonstop children, our home, and countless community and church volunteer jobs that keep my calendar booked till eternity. I can't be serious about the dreams inside of me. I'll just secretly work on my "to do" list for next week and everyone will think I'm paying attention.* I tried to tune Bill out.

But as I tried not to listen, something he said struck a responsive chord deep within me. It was Psalm 37:4-6.

> *Delight yourself in the LORD*
> *and he will give you the desires of your heart.*
>
> *Commit your way to the LORD;*
> *trust in him and he will do this:*
> *He will make your righteousness shine like the dawn,*
> *the justice of your cause like the noonday sun.*

I sat mesmerized as Bill suggested that if we are people who want to delight ourselves in the Lord, people who want to please and obey God, then the desires of our heart may have been placed there by God for a reason. The very dreams within us could be keys to understanding why God put us here on planet earth at this particular time in history. In other words, Bill asked us to believe, even if we could believe only with poppy-seed-size faith, that God plants His dreams and desires in His people.

Then Bill gave us an assignment. He asked each of us to go off somewhere and write down the ten most wonderful things God could do with us for the rest of our life—the dreams or desires that we've always wanted to pursue. He instructed us not to let anything limit our dreams—not education, finances, location, age, or any kind of circumstances. We were just to permit ourselves to think about what we would really like to do if there were nothing holding us back.

I landed on a bench under a wise-looking, aged oak tree and began my list. I was embarrassed at the thought of sharing it openly because my dreams seemed so grand—totally beyond reach. I laughed aloud at myself when I read the first two items on my list.

My first dream was to write a book. I looked at the sky and daydreamed again for a moment. I traveled back to the clubhouse I built in my backyard when I was a child. There I had created and written a neighborhood newspaper. I used my father's carbon paper to make copies that I sold for a nickel each.

I also thought about how, for a quarter of a century, I had collected hundreds of ideas, journaled countless stories, and recorded principle after principle I was learning, usually the hard way, about child raising, family life, and womanhood. I did this for my own benefit, but in the back of my mind I hoped to share what I was learning with other women somehow. "Yes," I confirmed aloud, "I do have a deep desire to write." I got goose bumps just thinking about it!

My second desire was to speak to large groups of women. I fantasized about standing on a stage in front of five hundred women. I could feel the excitement of their listening, their laughter, and their hunger to learn God's truth. "Oh, what an incredible privilege that would be! But it's all right, Lord, if I never get to do that," I prayed in unbelief. "Just keep me in Your speaker file if You ever need someone to fill a spot."

• •

The moment you alter your perception of yourself and your future, both you and your future begin to change.

—MARILEE ZDENEK, *INC. YOUR DREAMS*

Growth Op

What have you always wanted to pursue? Write down the ten most wonderful things God could do with you, for you, through you, in you, for the rest of your life—the dreams or desires that you've always wanted to pursue. And remember, don't let any obstacle hinder your dreams—education, finances, location, age, or any kind of circumstances.

Look up the following Scripture references and think about what they mean to you: Exodus 33:14, Psalm 56:13, Proverbs 4:11, John 16:13, Revelation 7:17.

The retreat ended, and we returned to the real world of laundry, leaky faucets, and bills. Six weeks passed, but I couldn't get my list of desires off my mind. I thought about them at night when I couldn't sleep, in the morning when I got up, in the car while I was driving. I decided to step out and do what was within my power to make some of these dreams come true. I asked God to do His part if He wanted them to happen. I prayed that He would open doors for me to speak, and I decided to write a book.

I approached Bill with his usual Saturday "honey-do" list, only this time I added a little something extra. I asked him to fix the front door, clean out the garage, caulk the tub, and publish a book. "Publish a book!" he exclaimed. "What do you mean, publish a book?"

"Now look," I firmly replied, "you got me into this! I'm just following your advice and getting in touch with the dreams and desires within my heart." We spent hours talking and praying.

Finally, swallowing hard, Bill couldn't deny it. He acquiesced and said, "Okay, here's two thousand dollars, the sum total of our savings. Please try not to lose it."

It was the first of January when I started thinking about what felt needs all moms have in common. *Summer*, I thought. *Every mother in the United States pulls her hair out during the summer. This would be a great time to start creating a fun, family atmosphere.* The next three months flew by. Writing; editing; choosing typeface; laying out the pages; deciding on interior art, paper, and binding; finding cover art—we learned a lot fast about self-publishing. The first copies of *A Mother's Manual for Summer Survival* rolled off the press March 31, 1988.

• •

I learned this, at least by my experiment: that if one advances confidently in the direction of his dreams, and endeavors to love the life which he has imagined, he will meet with a success unexpected in common hours.

—HENRY DAVID THOREAU

Thrilled to have the actual product in hand, I hopped in my car and drove to Dallas. I stopped at the city limits, found a pay phone, and looked up "Bookstores" in the yellow pages. I chose the six best advertisements and headed for those stores.

Trying to look as calm and professional as possible, I walked into each store and said, "Hi! I'm Kathy Peel and this is *A Mother's Manual for Summer Survival*. I think every mom who walks into your store will buy this book. How many would you like to order?"

Well, shock of my life, they all wanted to buy the book! I didn't even know how much to charge for it. Thankfully, the first gracious bookstore manager helped me figure out a price that would allow us both to make some money.

The fact that we had created something people thought was worth buying was too good to be true. Realizing this little project might just be bigger than we anticipated, I drove home in a twilight-zone state. When I got there, Bill and I sat down at the kitchen table and wrote a homespun marketing plan. Shortly after implementing it, we began to receive orders regularly. After only nine weeks we sold fifteen thousand copies.

I decided we needed some national exposure, so I mailed our overnight success story and a copy of the book to the major networks. Amazingly, CNN picked it up. After our story was featured five times within a twenty-four hour period on CNN, we began to receive phone calls from mothers across the United States and five foreign countries. The word *distribution* took on new meaning in our lives. It didn't take long to figure out we needed help.

I approached a friend who knew people in the publishing industry and asked if he could help us find a publisher. Six months later we had a contract with Focus on the Family Publishing. They helped us rewrite and expand our book to be rereleased in spring of 1989.

> Faith is the daring of the soul to go farther than it can see.
>
> —WILLIAM NEWTON CLARKE

A Mother's Manual for Summer Survival became an instant best seller. (To date it has sold over 350,000 copies.) What started as a poppy-seed-size step of faith has resulted in two corporations committed to providing creative resources to strengthen busy families. Twelve books, several videos, columns in five magazines, dozens of seminars, TV appearances, and countless radio interviews later, I am living out my dreams.

Bill taught me that God is big enough and cares enough about me to help me discover His plans for me. But, perhaps even more importantly, he taught me that the incredible rush of pleasure I feel after turning in a manuscript or speaking to a large group of women is the smile of God in my life. When we discover our destiny, find what God created us to do, it pleases Him, producing an inner joy in us that comes directly from employing His gifts. I always loved how Eric Liddell, the runner in *Chariots of Fire*, put it: "When I run fast, I feel His pleasure."

Growth Op

When do you feel God's pleasure? How could you feel it more often or in greater degrees?

God Gives Us What We Need

In Ephesians 2:10, the apostle Paul tells us, "For we are God's work-manship, created in Christ Jesus to do good works, which God pre-pared in advance for us to do." I didn't acquire these gifts myself. Yes, it's true I would rather write a magazine article than bake a cake. But this is the way God put me together. He had certain accomplishments in mind when He created me, and He gave me the equipment I needed to do the work. Using God's gifts to do God's will brings me the greatest pleasure imaginable.

• •

Whatever it is, however impossible it seems, whatever the obstacles that stand between you and it, if it is noble, if it is consistent with God's kingdom, you hunger after it, if you must stretch yourself to reach it.

—CHARLES COHN

We can only speculate as to what happened in Nehemiah's life leading up to the time when he stretched to reach his dream. Maybe when he was a boy, his dad was part of the king's carpentry crew, and Nehemiah watched and helped him plan, measure, and build items for the king. Maybe as a young man, as part of his own servi-tude, he was in charge of a palace remodeling project. So when this grand wall-building dream appeared on the horizon of his mind, maybe he felt confident that he could pull it off. Or maybe he was more intimidated by this dream than he'd ever been in his entire life.

We Can Count on God

We can indeed count on God to guide us, which is the crucial point of this chapter, just as Nehemiah could. But it's important to remember that Nehemiah prayed and fasted for a

• •

You must do the thing you think you cannot do.

—ELEANOR ROOSEVELT

long time before he knew exactly what he was to do, not to mention begin to do it. The problem is, in our culture we desire easy, instant answers to life's knottiest questions. In a day when our cultural heroes and television celebrities solve life's dilemmas in thirty to sixty minutes, we would love to dial an 800 number for instant access to someone who knew what he or she was talking about. We want immediate answers to questions like:

⟶ What should I do with my life?

⟶ Should I change jobs?

⟶ Should I take this promotion?

⟶ Should I marry? Whom should I marry?

⟶ Should I have children?

⟶ Should I follow this dream?

⟶ Should I take this new risk?

The search for immediate answers is not new, although maybe it's more widespread in these days of instant communications, nor is the search for answers from psychic gurus of one sort or another. As the following passage from Job reveals, only one person understands the way to wisdom: He who sees everything under the heavens, including into our hearts.

> *Where then does wisdom come from?*
> *Where does understanding dwell?*
> *It is hidden from the eyes of every living thing,*
> *concealed even from the birds of the air.*
> *Destruction and Death say,*
> *"Only a rumor of it has reached our ears."*
> *God understands the way to it*
> *and he alone knows where it dwells,*
> *for he views the ends of the earth*
> *and sees everything under the heavens.*
> *(Job 28:20-24)*

If we're going to seek a guide, it stands to reason that we need to find someone who's already been there. The only one we know who has been into tomorrow is the sovereign God of the future Himself.

● ●

What we really need to have is the Guide himself. Maps, road signs, a few useful phrases are good things, but infinitely better is someone who has been there before and knows the way.

—ELISABETH ELLIOT, AMERICAN AUTHOR

Those of us who know Christ don't consult the stars. We look to the One who made them. We can't pick up a book and find three specific steps to take toward our destiny, or pick up a magazine with God's will next to the horoscopes. We can't call a hot line and expect God to speak. He's a Person to be followed, not a magical problem solver we turn to on the spur of the moment and ignore in our daily lives. If we want God to give us direction, we have to decide to live for Him. He'll take care of the rest; it is His very nature to guide. In Psalm 23, David reminds us that the Lord, after all, is a shepherd.

The LORD is my shepherd, I shall not be in want.
He makes me lie down in green pastures,
he leads me beside quiet waters,
he restores my soul.
He guides me in paths of righteousness
for his name's sake.
Even though I walk
through the valley of the shadow of death,
I will fear no evil,
for you are with me;
your rod and your staff,
they comfort me. (Psalm 23:1-4)

God Still Guides Us

The world we live in is certainly a far cry from that of David or Nehemiah. Is it reasonable to expect that God will guide us through the tangle and confusion of modern life? If God is a shepherd, then He certainly does want to lead us. He always has and always will. His guidance is not only something we long for, it is a historic fact. Listen to just a couple of the promises of the Bible.

> *In your unfailing love you will lead*
> *the people you have redeemed.*
> *In your strength you will guide them*
> *to your holy dwelling. (Exodus 15:13)*

> *I will lead the blind by ways they have not known,*
> *along unfamiliar paths I will guide them;*
> *I will turn the darkness into light before them*
> *and make the rough places smooth.*
> *These are the things I will do;*
> *I will not forsake them. (Isaiah 42:16)*

Even though the future might be frightening, even though our dreams might actually send us into a terror when we think about actually stepping out and moving toward them, we can be confident that there is a Guide, One who goes before us and leads the way. Since He's eternal, the past, present, and future are all the same to the Lord Jesus Christ, and He constantly stretches out His hand toward us from the future and asks us to reach into His hands and let Him lead the way. Rest assured, you're never alone.

God's Means of Guiding His Children

Throughout history, God has used a variety of methods to lead and guide His children, some of which were quite spectacular. He used a burning bush to get Moses' attention, a cloud and fire to guide the Jews through the wilderness, a star to bring the wise men to

Bethlehem. Often God led through an audible, supernatural voice, or a visible appearance to those He wanted to lead, such as Abraham or Joshua. Sometimes God sent angels, His heavenly messengers, to bring instructions to His people — and on occasion to the ungodly. The Bible records so many appearances of angels that it's hard to count them. Another way God has led human beings is through supernatural dreams and visions. More than 150 times, the Bible talks about God giving dreams to people in the night to guide them. Less dramatic than angels or visions, ordinary people have carried God's message — like the prophets of both Testaments. And as we've mentioned, at times He even used animals, such as Balaam's donkey, to deliver His message.

Some days it would be really wonderful to get one of those visible, decisive indications of what God really wants us to do. Sometimes we would like that kind of clarity: guidance as clear as a stoplight — red light, you stop; green light, you go — no debate, no discussion. We should note two things about supernatural means of guidance, however. First, most of the time when God uses dramatic means of delivering His message, it was not sought, and when it was, it was not necessarily accepted. Receiving a miraculous message was no real help to people in following God's guidance — the guidance may have been clear, but they still had to *follow* it. Second, the people who received these supernatural messages were going about their usual business when God broke in on them. They were not waiting for something supernatural to happen. They were engaged in their daily work. In many of the instances when God spoke to or guided His people in some miraculous way, it was almost always at His discretion rather than an answer to someone seeking a miraculous sign.

The way we believe that God speaks to us most often is through *quiet, inaudible whispers in our heart* as we are going about our daily business. Even during times when God dramatically revealed Himself more frequently, most of the time He led people in this quiet way. Listen to these testimonies:

> *I will praise the Lord, who counsels me;*
> *even at night my heart instructs me. (Psalm 16:7)*

I guide you in the way of wisdom
and lead you along straight paths. (Proverbs 4:11)

This is exactly how God led Nehemiah toward his destiny — no angels, no pillars of cloud, no burning bushes — just quiet impressions in his heart. Fortunately, Nehemiah recognized God's whisper and followed the intimations he received. If he had been waiting for some dramatic message or supernatural confirmation, the walls of Jerusalem would never have been rebuilt.

Five Facts About Our Destiny

He is a wise man who wastes no energy on the pursuits for which he is not fitted; and he is still wiser who, from the things he can do well, chooses and resolutely follows the best.

WILLIAM GLADSTONE, BRITISH STATESMAN

Do what you know best; if you're a runner, run, if you're a bell, ring.

IGNAS BERNSTEIN

Ever since he was a young boy, a man we'll call Jim dreamed of building bridges and highways, so his goal was to get a degree in civil engineering. Then one day in church the pastor preached on 2 Peter 3:10: "But the day of the Lord will come like a thief. The heavens will disappear with a roar; the elements will be destroyed by fire, and the earth and everything in it will be laid bare."

Here's what Jim pictured as he listened to the sermon: He would spend his life building bridges, then the Lord would burn them up. The point of the sermon was clear. Temporal things are ultimately valueless. Suddenly a civil engineering degree sounded like a waste of time, and he decided to change majors and go to seminary. Now Jim spends his time as a church administrator, but he still dreams about building bridges. Was he following his God-given destiny or a misapplication of a Bible verse?

Like Jim, many of us have developed some strange ideas about God's will—not just how it's discovered, but what it is. Sometimes we get these strange ideas by mistake, like Jim did, from well-meaning pastors or teachers. Some of us inherited a fire-and-brimstone idea of a God who isn't happy unless we're suffering. Some have concocted a sugar-plum-fairy sort of God who isn't happy unless our every wish is fulfilled, immediately if not sooner, and never mind at whose expense. And some mistake the wounding of our early childhood—psychological or physical hurts inflicted on us by adults who should have known better (sometimes even in the name of God)—as God's doing. What we really need to do is consider the facts.

Fact One:
God's Will Embraces a Wide Variety of Needs and Opportunities

Christians often draw a distinction between what is eternal and what is temporal, things of the world and things of heaven. Perhaps you've been told that two things are eternal—the Word of God and the souls of men. Everything else will burn up. The implication is this: If you spend your time and your energy on anything other than these two things, then, quite frankly, as far as God is concerned, you are wasting your time. Yes, Scripture says in the end everything of this world will burn, but it also says that "God saw all that he had made, and it was very good" (Genesis 1:31) and "The earth is full of the goodness of the LORD" (Psalm 33:5, KJV).

We often hear that our destiny involves only spiritual things. Is this religious-sounding outlook biblical? Didn't God create the physical world as well as the spiritual? Stop to consider what wonderful blessings roads and bridges are to God's people — before they're burned up, that is. Think about Nehemiah. Was his preoccupation with rebuilding the walls of Jerusalem a colossal waste, given the fact that they would burn up one day? Could it be that God's interests extend much further than simply the spiritual welfare of His people?

Even though the world outside the four walls of the church is largely dominated by worldly thinking, we cannot assume that God is not interested in that part of His creation. The very fact that worldly thinking has so often invaded the church might give us a clue that it's possible for spiritual thinking to reinvade those realms the world has claimed by squatter's rights. The fact is, God's work in His world includes a whole variety of activities, meeting legitimate needs, whether they're spiritual, physical, or emotional. And He wants His children to dream grand dreams about doing great things in all of these areas. Whether you are building bridges or building people, God wants you to do all things for His glory. The apostle Paul makes it very clear that we can make *whatever* we do — even the most menial task — an act of worship.

> *Whatever you do, work at it with all your heart, as working for the Lord, not for men, since you know that you will receive an inheritance from the Lord as a reward. It is the Lord Christ you are serving.* (Colossians 3:23-24)

People who would like to divide the world up into the secular versus the sacred forget that a full 75 percent of the men and women we consider biblical heroes "wasted their time" in "secular" jobs for most of their lives. Look at the job descriptions for these eight Bible heroes and see how spiritual they sound to you. Can you identify them by their "secular" accomplishments?

➤ He left his family estate to move west and eventually built a sizable livestock empire on the open range.

➤ Reared in the family ranching business, his jealous brothers had him kidnapped and taken to a foreign country where he eventually rose to a top governmental position and saved the Near East from famine by savvy grain futures trading.

➤ In a day when women were considered baby factories, she executed several entrepreneurial ventures into real estate and textiles, while maintaining excellent management of her family estate.

➤ Taken hostage as a teenager by a tyrannical government, he resisted brainwashing and rose to the top in government service, becoming chief advisor to several successive regimes, serving kings well into his eighties.

➤ Son of a humble sheep rancher, he was a musical prodigy, and to the surprise of all he became a great military hero and later the supreme ruler of his country.

➤ During his rise to international renown, he made significant contributions in agriculture, architecture, and literature. He was hand-selected by his father to carry out the most important building project of his land.

➤ He had the most promising young mind in the Jewish legal community. Later, he made a career move into the manufacture of portable housing, allowing him greater flexibility in his ministry.

➠This career bureaucrat became the general contractor over a large government rehabilitation project. He overcame sabotage, an international acquisition nightmare, an inadequate labor force, and resisted profiteering and under-the-table deals to bring the job in ahead of schedule.

Did you recognize Abraham, Joseph, the Proverbs 31 "ideal" woman, Daniel, David, Solomon, Paul, and, of course, Nehemiah? Could these individuals have missed God's best—missed their destiny? In fact, it is possible that Jesus spent close to 90 percent of His earthly life "wasting His time" wielding a hammer. On the contrary, *all work is God's work—unless the work itself is sinful.*

God has not limited Himself to working just inside the church, and He does not want His children to limit their dreams to prayer, Bible study, evangelism, and other "spiritual" matters. His will includes meeting a whole gamut of legitimate physical, emotional, intellectual, social, as well as spiritual needs. As a matter of fact, all of these needs fall into the realm of the spiritual because they were all created by God. The only areas that would not be considered spiritual and are automatically off limits are those actions and attitudes the Bible calls sin.

Actually, what makes a dream sacred or secular, valuable or worthless, pleasing or unpleasing to God has more to do with our attitude and

Growth Op

Do any of the following ring a bell for you? Add your own suggestions to the list, even if they don't seem like "God's work."

➠Starting a nonprofit foundation to help illiterate adults learn to read

➠Remodeling a historic building and opening a restaurant

➠Spending a year in Africa as a missionary

➠Owning a retreat home in the country to enjoy creation with your family

➠Training for and running in the Boston Marathon

➠Starting a computer-generated special-effects company

➠Running for political office

motive than with what the job entails. A religious-appearing enterprise can be worthless before God if our motives are self-serving or our actions are abusive of others.

What this means is that if we dream about building bridges, we'd better take that as a clue to our destiny. If we dream about teaching people God's Word, we'd better consider seminary. But we can't fall into the trap of thinking one is more significant to God than the other. Our motives need to be checked in either case.

Fact Two:
Finding Our Destiny Sometimes Means Saying No to Good Things

Feed the Masses, Bibles Across the Border, Operation Vaccination, Inner-city Food Bank, Evangelize the World—every day we are bombarded by television, newspaper, and magazine ads and bulk-rate, voice, and e-mail with requests for our time, money, and energy to help a worthy cause. There are thousands of voices calling to us, asking for help. If we respond to every one, there won't be enough of us to go around.

There are people whose calendars are booked till eternity because they've said yes to everyone who has asked them to do anything. This is not a good idea, for at least two reasons. First, there's only so much one person can do well. And second, we risk burnout—getting to the point where we can't do much at all. We must learn to say no, but how can we decide what to turn down?

Some things are clear. Each of us has a compelling responsibility to other members of the body of Christ. James reminds us:

> *What good is it, my brothers, if a man claims to have faith but has no deeds? Can such faith save him? Suppose a brother or sister is without clothes and daily food. If one of you says to him, "Go, I wish you well; keep warm and well fed," but does nothing about his*

physical needs, what good is it? In the same way, faith by itself, if it is not accompanied by action, is dead. (James 2:14-17)

What we do know about God's will is this: If a brother has a legitimate immediate need and we have the means to meet that need, then we have an obligation to do so on a short-term basis. We don't need to pray about it or seek God's will about it. He's already revealed it. We just need to do it. Each person has certain family responsibilities within the body of Christ he or she is obliged to meet. We may not have the gift of hospitality, but if our neighbor's house burns down, we have an obligation to be hospitable and offer shelter, if needed. If a friend's child has an automobile accident and must have extensive surgery to live, and the friend loses his job as a result of missing so many days at work, we may not have the gift of giving, but if we can help financially we should.

Even though, according to James, my faith compels me to meet immediate emergency needs, I am not required to open a homeless shelter or start a food bank just because there's a need. A need does not always constitute a call. But how do we recognize God's call? Our dreams help us discover where we should invest ourselves and our resources.

> He who is not liberal with what he has does but deceive himself when he thinks he would be liberal if he had more.
>
> —W. S. Tulner

No doubt Nehemiah found great satisfaction in his new career as a wall builder. If Jim were building bridges, perhaps he wouldn't spend work time dreaming about something else. And, after all, isn't idling away time at work a form of stealing? Surely that's not God's destiny for us. We can, of course, in the short run, fool ourselves into thinking that we're seeking our destiny when what we're really seeking is our pleasure. A quest for self-fulfillment and pleasure is nothing short of hedonism. But we need to trust ourselves and God. If we're seeking pleasure, the feeling is *not* going to last, and soon we'll be on to the next thing, and the next, and our search becomes frantic. When we're feeling truly fulfilled,

Growth Op

Make a list of five things people have asked you to do that are *not* calls from God. Then make a list of five things those first ones bring to mind that might be calls from God.

it's a good clue that we're finding God's destiny for us.

Without some direction, we are likely to fall victim to the person with the most compelling story or most persuasive personality—not a good way to discover our destiny or determine how to invest our resources. Or worse, without a way to sort through needs, we might stop short of action—"I can't do everything so I'll do nothing." Now that's hedonistic.

Fact Three:
God's Will and My Dreams Are Not in Automatic Conflict

All of us, at times, dream with selfish motives about sinful things. But this doesn't necessarily mean all of our dreams are suspect to God. Just because we want to do something badly does not put it in conflict, by default, with what God wants. If the dream is good, right, and noble, we should consider the possibility that God planted the dream in us.

Many Christians have a lingering mistrust of their own dreams and the things that seem to be personally satisfying. Their thinking goes something like this: *There are God's desires and my desires, and they never run in the same direction. In other words, if I want something badly, it surely isn't God's will for me to have it. That would be too good to be true.*

Small wonder so many people fear God's will as something that will, more than likely, make them miserable. Sadly, it dawns on few of us when we cut our spiritual teeth that God might put desires in our hearts as a way of guiding our hands and feet. The fact is, God loves us more than we can possibly imagine, cares infinitely about our lives, and very often wants the same good things we do. In fact,

if doing God's will is our priority, we can count on the One who created us and loves us more than we love ourselves to let us know
which direction to take.

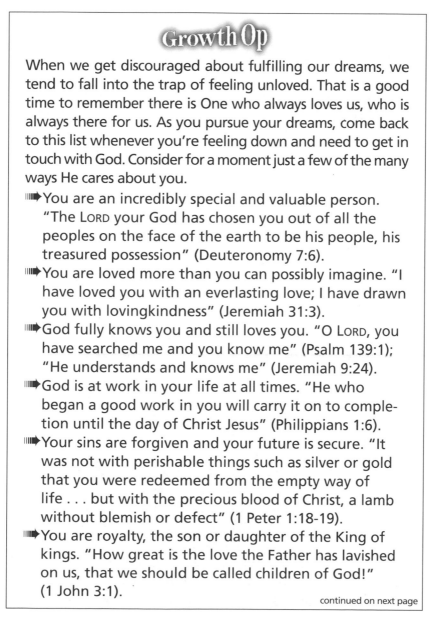

Growth Op

When we get discouraged about fulfilling our dreams, we
tend to fall into the trap of feeling unloved. That is a good
time to remember there is One who always loves us, who is
always there for us. As you pursue your dreams, come back
to this list whenever you're feeling down and need to get in
touch with God. Consider for a moment just a few of the many
ways He cares about you.

➠ You are an incredibly special and valuable person.
"The LORD your God has chosen you out of all the
peoples on the face of the earth to be his people, his
treasured possession" (Deuteronomy 7:6).

➠ You are loved more than you can possibly imagine. "I
have loved you with an everlasting love; I have drawn
you with lovingkindness" (Jeremiah 31:3).

➠ God fully knows you and still loves you. "O LORD, you
have searched me and you know me" (Psalm 139:1);
"He understands and knows me" (Jeremiah 9:24).

➠ God is at work in your life at all times. "He who
began a good work in you will carry it on to completion until the day of Christ Jesus" (Philippians 1:6).

➠ Your sins are forgiven and your future is secure. "It
was not with perishable things such as silver or gold
that you were redeemed from the empty way of
life . . . but with the precious blood of Christ, a lamb
without blemish or defect" (1 Peter 1:18-19).

➠ You are royalty, the son or daughter of the King of
kings. "How great is the love the Father has lavished
on us, that we should be called children of God!"
(1 John 3:1).

continued on next page

continued from previous page

➠You are a uniquely designed, one-of-a-kind work of art. "For you created my inmost being; you knit me together in my mother's womb. I praise you because I am fearfully and wonderfully made" (Psalm 139:13-14).

➠You are designed for a purpose. "The people I formed for myself that they may proclaim my praise" (Isaiah 43:21).

➠You are continually sustained and protected. "Cast your cares on the LORD and he will sustain you; he will never let the righteous fall" (Psalm 55:22).

➠You are never alone. "For the LORD your God will be with you wherever you go" (Joshua 1:9).

➠You are under God's constant care. "Cast all your anxiety on him because he cares for you" (1 Peter 5:7).

➠You are God's responsibility. "You did not choose me, but I chose you and appointed you to go and bear fruit—fruit that will last. Then the Father will give you whatever you ask in my name" (John 15:16).

➠You are a work of art, a masterpiece—created by God Himself. "For we are God's workmanship, created in Christ Jesus to do good works, which God prepared in advance for us to do" (Ephesians 2:10).

• •

Jesus said, "I came that they might have life, and might have it abundantly."

—JOHN 10:10, NASB

God's will is not something that automatically turns us 180 degrees from what we want to do, unless it is sinful. Following God's will is essentially and fundamentally being what we were made to be, which also brings us the greatest sense of fulfillment and joy. Far from wanting to make our lives miserable, God wants us to find our greatest joy, which is to do the very things He created us for. As His creature, even after the Fall, we move toward that instinctively. The delight we feel when we're doing the things He created us to do is not the selfish delight of our flesh (unless the acts are sinful by nature), but His smile on our lives as we do His work.

In Genesis 1 and 2 Adam and Eve were doing what God designed them to do—cultivating the garden, ruling over the animals, and enjoying each other's intimacy—yet there's no mention of verbal praise. God was pleased with His creation and said so at the end of the day in the strongest terms possible—"God saw all that he had made, and it was very good." Everything, including man, was doing what it was created to do, and by doing so brought glory to God in a symphony of praise. The acts of obedience themselves were wordless acclamations.

• •

Work is the natural exercise and function of man. . . . Work is not primarily a thing one does to live, but the thing one lives to do. It is, or should be, the full expression of the worker's faculties, the thing in which he finds spiritual, mental and bodily satisfaction, and the medium in which he offers Himself to God.

—DOROTHY SAYERS, BRITISH WRITER

The Real Conflict

Unfortunately, when man and woman chose to live life according to their own design, humankind became the only part of God's creation that tries to be something it's not and does things for which it was not created. And worse than that, even when we choose to be what we are and do things for which we were created, we can be and do these things for the wrong reason—to glorify ourselves.

The world is full of individuals who want to enlist God's aid in fulfilling their dreams and selfish agendas. But don't think your dreams are by nature selfish just because you passionately desire them. The biggest problem is not a conflict of wills—my plan versus God's. Nor is it always about *what* I'm doing. Often the biggest

<table>
<tr><td>

Growth Op

Can you honestly believe God would have you do something or lead you somewhere that was not in your best interests? Contemplate the idea that He loves you enough to guide you to the place where you will find the greatest satisfaction and joy possible. What might your life be like if you acted as if you believed this?

</td></tr>
</table>

• •

Enemy-occupied territory—that is what this world is. Christianity is the story of how the rightful King has landed in disguise, and is calling us all to take part in a great campaign of sabotage.

—C. S. LEWIS

problem is *why* I'm doing something. Many of us struggle more with our motives than with our sense of direction. The ugliest thing about any of us is the compulsive, "me-centered" use of the gifts and opportunities God gave us for the expression of our destiny. We may be doing the right thing, but fail to consider *God's* timing and *God's* glory. We can be sure, though, that if our motivation is to indulge ourselves rather than glorify God, then what could have been a wonderfully satisfying experience may bring a moment of pleasure, but it will ultimately bring us nothing but disappointment.

The Lord Jesus' call to "deny yourself, take up your cross daily, and follow me" is not a call to give up our deepest longings and resign ourselves to emptiness. Rather, it is a call to abandon our quest for self-fulfillment on *our* terms and in *our* timing. When we offer our gifts and dreams to God to serve Him, often we find that they are the very things He wants us to pursue—in His timing and for His glory.

Fact Four:
Something Is Wrong with You
If You Don't Dream

If you are presently comfortable in your circumstances, don't assume there's no need to seek your destiny. Dreaming is not only for discontented people. The world we live in is not the world that God intended, and we can never be fully content with the way things are until Jesus returns to reestablish His kingdom on earth. Until that time, there will always be enemy territory to retake. God plans to retake the world He created and restore the wondrous beauty of His creation—and we're part of the plot to overthrow Satan's domination.

Even when Christ returns, however, we believe men and women will still dream. When God put Adam and Eve on the earth, He commissioned them to fill the earth and subdue it. They began a grand development program that, although thwarted and misdirected by Satan, nonetheless goes on and will continue. When Christ returns, we personally don't see the world returning to subsistence living under His reign, but rather human genius unleashed from sin's limitations and abuses. There will be new technologies, new discoveries, new advances that even techno-geniuses in the Silicon Valley can't fathom.

The short and long of it is that if we don't dream, we have nothing to strive for. When we stop dreaming and reaching, our God-given talents don't lie in some bank gaining interest so we can use them when we need them. On the contrary, when we stop pursuing dreams and "impossibilities," our souls dry up. Despair moves into the desert of our hearts. Then, all because we didn't dare to dream when we were in comfortable circumstances, suddenly we can't dream when we need a dream most.

GrowthOp

Can you pinpoint a time in your life when you stopped dreaming? What ideas and talents have you stored away? Can you sense God calling you to get something out of mothballs?

Fact Five:
Pursuing Our Destiny Is Anything But Easy

Living a life of destiny is not the quest for safe waters. Look at the men and women of the Bible who followed hard after God and you'll see lives often checkered with not only suffering, but also failure. Men and women who have found God's path can still fall in the ditch morally, be accosted by enemies, or find themselves in a hailstorm of circumstances. In fact, for some God's path is a steep mountain trail, paved with jagged boulders. Some never reach the peak.

What one does find in pursuing one's destiny is a deep, God-given satisfaction that comes only from the warm smile of God on the life that is doing what God created it to do. It is a satisfaction and joy that is oblivious to pain and ultimately even to the success of the venture. The joy is in the journey — God's journey.

Wherever you are today, finding the path and discovering your destiny is worth the search.

Growth Op

Read Hebrews 11 from a modern translation of the Bible.

CHAPTER 6

Passion:
Your Personal
North Star

*Without passion man is a mere latent
force and possibility, like the flint which
awaits the shock of the iron before it can
give forth its spark.*

HENRI-FREDERIC AMIEL, SWISS PHILOSOPHER

*Passion, though a bad regulator,
is a powerful spring.*

RALPH WALDO EMERSON

The hotel banquet hall was packed. All eyes were on the speaker. The doctor closed his compelling talk on missions to young medical students with this challenge: "If you haven't been called to stay, then you must go!"

God had powerfully used this man to impact both the spiritual and bodily health of a small Third World country. His challenge to consider medical missions as a career was a challenge to be reckoned with, and since I spend a lot of time with medical students, I could look around the room and tell it hit them hard in the heart. But was the doctor right about God's call?

Bob, a second-year medical student, phoned the next week with a boatload of questions about God's calling. Bob wondered if it was wrong that he desired to stay in the States and practice medicine with his dad.

Jim had been on a short-term medical mission trip the summer before he entered medical school, and this experience had intensified his desire to help people. But he didn't feel a strong internal tug pulling him to channel his energies in that direction. Was he being selfish? Unspiritual? Was he out of touch with God's will? Choosing second best?

Jan had the same questions. She sat at our table with her head hung low. She had attended the same lecture and afterward was so excited she almost burst. From the time she was in college, she had wanted to be a medical missionary. She even chose her medical school because of its proximity to one of the leading schools of tropical health. Jan's chosen course, however, had just been challenged by her sister, who told her she was just being self-centered. She should stay close to her family and forget this adventure. Jan was confused and guilt-ridden. Which voice was God's? Was she being selfish? True, she had loved adventure ever since she was a child. She also loved people from different cultures, felt drawn to them like a magnet. But she had a ferocious love for her family, who, for the most part, lived within a fifty-mile radius of each other. Was she just living for adventure? Or had God really called her to medical missions?

How can these three individuals, or anyone seeking direction, know which voice to listen to? For the Christian, this question is not just a matter of finding the most fulfilling vocation. It's an issue of obedience.

> The strength of a man consists in finding out the way God is going and going that way.
>
> —HENRY WARD BEECHER, AMERICAN THEOLOGIAN (1813–1887)

We have to decide which voice is from God. We can't do everything. So what is He calling us to do?

We believe there is a North Star for navigating the opportunities and needs that come our way. God has given us an internal compass. That compass is passion. Passion is given to guide us to God's will for our lives. Passion, however, has had some bad press and is often misunderstood. To some, the word *passion* brings back memories of illicit desires at drive-in movies with a high school flame. To others it evokes images of a murder committed in the height of rage. And it is true, passion is behind almost every sin. Remember what James tells us about passion (or "evil desire," as it's translated here)? "But each one is tempted when, by his own evil desire, he is dragged away and enticed" (James 1:14).

Actually, passion is morally neutral. It is simply a strong feeling or deep longing for something. When our passions or longings attach themselves to sinful objects, the Bible often calls them lusts or evil desires. However, passions and deep longings can also attach themselves to ideas and actions that are good. Consider King David's passion for the presence of God:

> *As the deer pants for streams of water,*
> *so my soul pants for you, O God. (Psalm 42:1)*

Or Paul's passion to be with Christ—"I am torn between the two: I *desire* to depart and be with Christ, which is better by far" (Philippians 1:23, emphasis added)—or his fellow believers: "But, brothers, when we were torn away from you for a short time (in person, not in thought), out of our *intense longing* we made every effort to see you" (1 Thessalonians 2:17, emphasis added). Even Christ had passion: "And he said to them, 'I have *eagerly desired* to eat this

Passover with you before I suffer'" (Luke 22:15, emphasis added).

Passion is the God-given ability to feel so deeply about something that it causes us to move toward the object of desire. This passion stems from an urge *given by God*—a burden, an emotional response to a need or opportunity He wants us to move toward. It's not a feeling that we experience and then lose easily. It's persistent and powerful. We can't ignore it.

> There is not a heart but has its moments of longing, yearning for something better, nobler, holier than it knows now.
>
> —HENRY WARD BEECHER, AMERICAN THEOLOGIAN

The Trailhead

Passion is the birthplace of a dream, the trailhead of a new path God wants us to follow. Passions are important for a number of reasons.

Passions Give Us Direction

They help us know where we want to go. They allow us to say yes with conviction and no without guilt. They provide us with a kind of nozzle to focus our energy. They keep us off the rabbit trails of life and on the main highway of God's unique purpose for us.

Each of us is constantly making tradeoffs with our time and energy—balancing the competing demands of family, work, friends, community, and our own personal needs. If we don't know our purpose, it will be easy to say yes too many times to too many requests, and the result will be imbalance, frustration, and ultimately burnout. Passion keeps our purpose clear before us.

If we find ourselves wanting to meet every need, then something is motivating us besides God. Guilt and the need for approval are both unmerciful taskmasters—"My mother always did this" or "Everyone else volunteered!" or a domineering person intimidated us into taking on something we're really not suited for.

God has not called us to meet every need. This brings a great deal of comfort to us as we seek to choose a path to follow. Each of us needs to realize that saying yes to one path automatically means saying no to another. If I'm prone to saying yes to every need I encounter, most often I'll say yes to the urgent rather than the important. By the time I get to what God really wants me to invest myself in, I'll be out of time and energy. But how can we distinguish between the urgent and important? And, even more crucial, how do we know specifically what God wants us to invest ourselves in? Passions point the way.

Kathy learned this principle in an interesting way. Because she writes books to strengthen families, sometimes she gets calls from people looking for a spokesperson to endorse a product or be a part of a family-image campaign. A few years ago a public relations firm contacted her for endorsement of a product we used and enjoyed in our home. Well, it sounded like a reasonable idea, in line with her passion to help women and strengthen families. And when they told her how much they would pay her, the job made a lot of sense. It was a lot of money. More money (for this one job) than we had seen in a full year. *Surely*, we thought, *God has placed this job in Kathy's path.*

The day came for Kathy to sign the contract. She flew to New York, was picked up by the company limo, and taken to the corporate headquarters. There she learned that the job description had changed from encouragement to adversarial debate. She was able to ask herself a simple question to determine if this was God's will. Would she be able to encourage and motivate women, and strengthen families? She realized the answer was no. So she left the check on the big rosewood table and five executives speechless. She knew this was not a path God wanted her to take.

We each need to stop to consider how we were individually created and what we feel passionate about before we head down a path. There are many strong personalities who think that their passion is the only thing God cares about. They have no scruples about using you as fuel for their cause. We must know if their activity is in harmony with our skills — our talents and expertise — and our passions. When skills and passions match a particular job or activity, we will

Growth Op

When have you said yes out of guilt or the need for approval? When someone asks you to volunteer for a good cause that is not your cause, or that you don't have the time, energy, or skills for right now, what could you say besides yes? (Hint: Sometimes four words are enough: "I'm sorry, I can't." Sometimes a more lengthy explanation is in order. But it all boils down to the same thing—no.)

be energized to do a great job. When passion and task don't match, the "opportunity" will take us down the road to burnout, and we'll do the job either poorly or not at all.

Passions Allow for Evaluation

Plato said, "The unexamined life is not worth living." But what will we measure our life by if we don't have a target? There's truth to the old adage that if we aim at nothing, we'll hit it every time. It's also true that if we shoot at everything in sight, we probably won't hit much. But then again, no one will know, because no one will know what we're really aiming at. By focusing on a target and evaluating the direction in which we are going, we can have some idea that we are getting somewhere.

• •

"Would you tell me, please, which way I ought to go from here?"

"That depends on where you want to get to," said the Cat.

"I don't much care where," said Alice.

"Then it doesn't matter which way you go," said the Cat.

"—so long as I get *somewhere*," Alice added as an explanation.

"Oh, you're sure to do that," said the Cat.

—Lewis Carroll, *The Annotated Alice Alice's Adventures in Wonderland and Through the Looking Glass*

Passion Ensures Resolve When Things Get Tough

Or as John Cameron Swayze said, "It takes a licking and keeps on ticking." "Ought's," "should's," and "good ideas" provide poor fuel for the crunch. Passion, on the other hand, provides an internal motivation to keep going when external rewards drop out of sight. When our heart has latched hold of what God wants us to do, we can stand a lot of pain and delayed gratification along the way, "for after a while we will reap a harvest of blessing if we don't get discouraged and give up" (Galatians 6:9, TLB). And we'll need that resolve because when we are traveling down the road toward God's dreams, we can be sure that there will be storms.

> Go on in fortune and misfortune like a clock in a thunderstorm.
>
> —ROBERT LOUIS STEVENSON

Passion is a renewable resource. It keeps going and going and going. How? We believe that God feeds it to keep us steadfast when obstacles appear.

> And let us not get tired of doing what is right, for after a while we will reap a harvest of blessing if we don't get discouraged and give up.
>
> —GALATIANS 6:9

The LORD is the everlasting God,
  the Creator of the ends
    of the earth.
He does not faint or grow weary,
  his understanding is
    unsearchable.
He gives power to the faint,
  and to him who has no
might he increases strength.
(Isaiah 40: 28-29, RSV)

Be glad for all God is planning for you. Be patient in trouble, and prayerful always. (Romans 12:12, TLB)

Growth Op

Nobody ever said it's easy to face a storm. Sometimes it helps to remind ourselves of times we were in stormy waters, or simply learning to do something new and afraid we'd fail. What are those times in your life? What are you confident doing now that you knew nothing about five years ago? We can use these instances to remind us of God's presence as we move out into new, uncharted waters.

Both strength

Discovering Your Passion

I am not afraid of storms for I am learning how to sail my ship.

—Louisa May Alcott

These, then, are some of the qualities of passion—why it's important to defining God's purpose for our life. The question now becomes: How do we get in touch with this passion? How do we discover the things that God wants us to feel really strongly about? We can look at how Nehemiah's passion came to him and see a paradigm as to how passions begin to manifest themselves in our hearts as well.

How do we know?

Passions come providentially. We can be sure that Hanani was on a mission from God, one that providentially brought this message about the state of Jerusalem some eight hundred miles to the man of His choice in His good time. This was no coincidence. God was at work to bring Nehemiah the information he needed to discover his destiny.

God is at work in the same way today, both within our hearts and behind the scenes of our lives, orchestrating events and directing people providentially, to bring us to the place He wants us to be. He is weaving a beautiful tapestry of events in our lives to lead us along supernaturally, and He never drops a stitch.

There is no such thing as a coincidence. What is God doing in your life right now? Whether you recognize it or not, He is preparing you for the destiny He has in mind for you on the road ahead.

Passions come naturally. Notice there was no burning bush, no angelic chorus, no thunderous announcement. The news about Jerusalem came to Nehemiah in the normal commerce of human communication. This is the way God speaks to most of us—through the everyday events of our lives. And yet, most of us are not listening because we don't expect God to speak to us in that way. If we're really listening though, like Nehemiah was, God would only have to whisper and we'd get the point. If we're waiting for burning bushes and dramatic signs to reveal God's will to us, we'll likely miss the still, quiet voice as we encounter the needs and opportunities that exist in the world around us.

Passions come emotionally. The *sine qua non* of passion is emotion. It's not something we work up, but something God plants in a receptive heart. God had certainly been at work in Nehemiah creating a passion for the people of Jerusalem and for the glory of His city. You can tell a lot about a person's passions by the questions he asks. Remember Nehemiah's question on Hanani's return from Jerusalem? Not "How was your trip?" or "Did you make a good profit?" or "How are Uncle Sol and Aunt Esther?" but "I questioned them about the Jewish remnant that survived the exile, and also about Jerusalem" (Nehemiah 1:2).

And when he heard this news, his heart was ready to respond—and it did, emotionally! Significantly, the size of our tears will determine the size of our work. Perhaps we should stop now and ask ourselves, What are we praying for? What is our passion? What do we cry over? What do we desire more than anything else?

God had providentially been at work to develop a deep concern for God's people and God's city in Nehemiah's heart. The extent of his response, however, was totally unexpected. He had certainly known, in general at least, the state of Jerusalem. After all, it had been in ruins since 586 B.C., almost 150 years. Yet, this time when he heard the news, it pricked his heart in a way it had never done before. Look at his response: "When I heard these things, I sat down and wept. For some days I mourned and fasted and prayed before the God of heaven" (1:4).

Passions come fearfully. Oftentimes, when men and women talk about understanding and knowing the will of God, they say peace is one of the things that God brings their way—that it is an indication that their dream is God's will. Quite frankly, it's comforting to read about Nehemiah's bout with fear, even if it was short-lived. He reports simply, "I was very much afraid" (2:2). The fact is that peace does not always accompany God's will. When our security is threatened, when what we are asked to do by God or begin thinking and dreaming about is bigger than anything else that we've ever imagined, fear will often be the result. So many people associate fear with sin, but fear is our human response to risk—not a sign that our dream is sinful.

Roadblocks to Passion

However, barriers can crop up and keep us from being passionate about God's will for our lives. Here are some of them:

Isolation from others' pain—If we draw our wagons in a circle and isolate and insulate ourselves from the world and its problems, we won't feel the pain. "Cocooning" is not only a market trend in our society, it is a reality for many American Christians. We might think we're safe from our increasingly hostile culture, shut up tight in our homes, but we're also safe from finding out the plan God has for our lives. It is possible to overinsulate ourselves if it keeps us from encountering the pain of the world around us that God wants to touch our heart.

Preoccupation with greed—More than likely, we are either preoccupied with our own greed or others' needs. The problem is that people wrapped up with themselves make awfully small packages, so small there's hardly room for anyone else, much less God. When we focus on ourselves, our needs seem so large that there is little emotional energy left to apply to someone else's welfare. When we as Christians allow this preoccupation, we are actually cutting ourselves off from enjoying the relationship with the one source of satisfaction and safety in this world—Jesus Christ. Not only does God command us to think of others as more important than ourselves, but we have every reason to do so. God guarantees our own needs will be met.

Burnout—When our emotional energy gets low, it short-circuits our ability to hear God. Someone warned us years ago,

If your output exceeds your intake,
Then your upkeep will be your downfall.

If you feel burned out right now, you're probably feeling numb about almost everything. Before you can be passionate and dream, you need to take time to refresh yourself.

Spiritual barriers—If we want to hear from God, we need to be listening. God has not obligated Himself to lead those who choose to walk their own path. If we have unconfessed sin in our lives, this could stand in our way of hearing God's voice in the circumstances of the day. If pride blunts our sensitivity to Him, or we're unwilling to deal with misdirected worldly passions, it is highly likely that we will miss His voice. If He is not our delight, how can He reveal His dreams to us, much less meet our deepest longings? Remember:

> *Delight yourself in the LORD*
> *and he will give you the desires of your heart.*
> *(Psalm 37:4)*

 ## Playing in Traffic

How do we go about finding God's destiny for our lives? Is there something we can do proactively to determine our God-given passion? According to Nehemiah's example, there are several actions we can take.

Be faithful right where we are. Where we are is God's purpose for us today until God says to move. There was certainly no indication of uneasiness, restlessness, and discontent in Nehemiah's life. He was absolutely committed to doing what he was supposed to be doing in the context of the present. His sense of the future did not distract him from the duties of the day. He was faithful in the little things God presented him with that day. And because he was faithful in small things, God could make him faithful in larger things as well. If you feel anxious, remember that in His timing God will bring you the information you need about where He wants you to go.

Focus on needs and opportunities, not greed. Put yourself in circulation. When World Vision puts the picture of a starving child on the television screen, look at it. Don't change the channel so that need and that pain won't invade your self-serving isolation and desire for comfort and safety. If we hole up in our cocoon, then we are putting ourselves in a position where it's awfully hard to hear God's voice. We need to allow ourselves to feel the pain. None of us should be afraid of pain. In fact, if we play in traffic, if we put ourselves in circulation, we can be sure we're going to be hit by something one day. It's not going to feel good.

Growth Op

To help determine your passions, which is the focal point of this chapter, ask yourself these questions.

1. What do I weep about? When I lie awake at night, what do I think about when I'm staring at the ceiling? What do I pound the table about?

2. What kind of issues, needs, opportunities, activities, ideas really motivate me and seem to give me energy?

3. If I could meet any need in the world, had every resource I needed, and knew I could not fail, what would I attempt to do? What need would I attempt to meet? What opportunity would I want to seize? What idea would I want to see come to fruition?

4. What things deeply concern me? Or what are the greatest opportunities in each of the following areas: My family life? My workplace? My church? My country? My community?

The only ability God really requires is availability. It doesn't take a big person to be used by God, a person with awesome skills or even spiritual maturity. What it takes is a person who is willing to be used, who says, "Lord, I am available to You. Use me as You want." Because Nehemiah felt that way, God was able to move into his heart, providentially bring him the news he needed, create the dream, and then move him toward the realization of his destiny. We believe that he wants to do the same with each of us. Dick Halverson, former chaplain of the U.S. Senate, said it well.

It doesn't take a big person to be used by God . . . but it does take all there is of him! You don't need a five-foot water pipe to irrigate a garden . . . you can do it with a quarter-inch hose . . . assuming an adequate source—a connection between it and the hose—and an uncluttered channel.[1]

7

Dreaming:
The Business
of Hope

Nothing happens unless first a dream.

CARL SANDBURG

Faith is the substance of things hoped for, the evidence of things not seen.

HEBREWS 11:1, KJV

NEW MEXICO—A young couple starts a family on a remote desert ranch, driving two hundred miles to El Paso, Texas, for the birth of their first child. They live in a four-room adobe house with no running water or electricity and no school within driving distance. But Harry and Ada Mae Day dream that their daughter might be able to go to Stanford University. They school her at home, subscribe to metropolitan newspapers and magazines, and later send her to the best boarding schools possible. Sandra did attend Stanford, then law school, and then became the first woman justice appointed to the Supreme Court of the United States.

TEXAS—Mary Kay Ash retires after twenty-five years with the same company. Although it was unusual then for a woman, she dreams of having her own company. So she invests her five-thousand-dollar life savings in herself and an idea for a cosmetics firm. In twenty years, her dream becomes a multimillion-dollar business. Mary Kay Cosmetics provides the opportunity for thousands of women to support themselves financially. More women earn over fifty thousand dollars a year at Mary Kay Cosmetics than at any other company in the world.

ALABAMA—A young black pastor dreams of a day when racial prejudice will be destroyed. He devotes his life to confronting racism in the United States. He mobilizes thousands of white and black Americans to join him in nonviolent civil disobedience of laws that are unjust to minority Americans. Because Martin Luther King, Jr., pursued his dream, American society was changed.

CALCUTTA—A diminutive, Albanian-born nun is burdened by the suffering in the streets of India. She dreams of a place where those who have nowhere else can go to die with dignity and forms the Missionaries of Charity in 1950. In 1979 she receives the Nobel Peace Prize for her work. Thousands of poor, suffering people know the love of Jesus Christ because of this woman known to the world simply as Mother Teresa.

• •

For the eyes of the Lord search back and forth across the whole earth, looking for people whose hearts are perfect toward him, so that he can show his great power in helping them.

—2 CHRONICLES 16:9, TLB

Dreaming is essential for every person who wants to know his or her destiny. It is serious business for people who want God's best for their lives. Of all people, it seems that men and women who profess to be Christians ought to understand the importance of entertaining substantial dreams. After all, we're the ones who have a big God who challenges us to call on Him in impossible situations.

This is what the LORD says, he who made the earth, the LORD who formed it and established it—the LORD is his name: "Call to me and I will answer you and tell you great and unsearchable things you do not know." (Jeremiah 33:2-3)

What Is a Dream?

Dreaming is one of the most powerful abilities God has conferred on the human race. But we're not talking about dreams in the night or supernatural visions. Nor are we speaking of a more typical form of dreaming in which all people, in all places, and in all eras have dreamed of change for the better, envisioning positive development, hoping for the improvement of something—whether it be a building, a relationship, a city, a country, a church, an organization, a person, a circumstance, whatever.

When we talk about a dream, we mean a God-given idea, plan, goal, or vision about a better future that He places in our mind. It's about seeing with our mind's eye the possibilities that something good can happen in the future, even when the world is dominated by malignant misery. It's about believing that God is at work enlightening the hearts of men and women so caught in darkness that they seem beyond hope of redemption. It's about believing great things will continue to happen, even in the midst of calamity, because God is great and good.

Dreaming, to put it plainly, is the *business of hope.*

• •

Hope is definitely not the same thing as optimism. It is not the conviction that something will turn out well, but the certainty that something makes sense, regardless of how it turns out.

—VÁCLAV HAVEL
FORMER PRESIDENT OF CZECHOSLAVAKIA

I was confronted with hope in a most unusual place — Oklahoma City. I traveled there to speak to more than five hundred men at a Promise Keepers Leadership conference and, after the conference, had the opportunity to drive through downtown. I stared in disbelief. What once had been the Alfred P. Murrah Federal Building was now an empty, grassy lot. All around were the signs of destruction. Fifty-one weeks after the Oklahoma City bombing, churches and office buildings surrounding the site still showed aftereffects of the blast. At 9:02 A.M. on April 19, 1995, a six-square-block area of downtown Oklahoma City, in the heartland of America, had been transformed into something resembling Beirut, Lebanon. I talked to a police captain who had been on the scene at 9:05. I talked to some who had just left the mayor's prayer breakfast two blocks away only moments before the blast. I talked to others whose family and friends hadn't been so fortunate. What amazed me was their hope. Their shock and grief had been replaced by a dream — a dream that in the midst of tragedy God would pour out His spirit on their city and turn this tragedy into triumph.

Dreaming is about seeing reality through God's eyes, unlimited by how someone else defines what is and isn't possible. It is about letting our imaginations run wild, beyond our own finite perceptions and limited abilities, and seeing the immeasurable possibilities defined by God's power.

Dreaming looks into the future and visualizes the world as God

• •

Make your plans as fantastic as you like, because 25 years from now, they will seem mediocre. Make your plans 10 times as great as you first planned, and 25 years from now you will wonder why you did not make them 50 times as great.

—HENRY CURTIS

meant it to be. We long for an ideal world because that is what we were created to live in. Dreaming puts color, texture, and details on the picture in our minds of the hope we have in Christ. He will personally recapture and redeem His fallen creation, and "he will wipe every tear from their eyes. There will be no more death or mourning or crying or pain, for the old order of things has passed away" (Revelation 21:4).

Dreams are important. We dream because God gave us the ability to dream. What do you dream about? If an immediate answer doesn't come to mind, that's okay. Let the question simmer on the back burner of your mind. Come back to it at a later date, but do come back.

The Value of Dreams

Dreams are absolutely essential for us personally, for society as well as for the kingdom of God. In fact, no one ever grows in Christ or pursues godliness without a dream—a dream of being what God created him or her to be. It could also be argued that every great step the human race has taken began with a dream. William Wilberforce dreamed of a day when every man in the British Empire would be free before he made a single impassioned plea in Parliament to abolish slavery. The apostle Paul dreamed of evangelizing Europe before he set one foot in Greece. As a young girl, Jane Addams saw poor children and dreamed of helping them. She founded Hull House in Chicago, a home for those without any. She continued her work on behalf of people everywhere and in 1931 won the Nobel Peace Prize. Thomas Edison dreamed of lighting a city with electric power before even the first of the seven thousand failures he committed on his way to inventing the electric light bulb. Before one package was ever delivered by Federal Express, Fred Smith, modern entrepreneur, dreamed of a fast, efficient system of getting packages from one place to another. These once impossible endeavors sprouted from the seeds of dreams.

"The LORD your God will be with you wherever you go."

—JOSHUA 1:9

Radical Dependence

Radical dreams make us radically dependent. As we said in chapter 2, God has called us not merely to *be* something, but also to *do* something. And in His Word, He has promised assistance in that task.

When we engage in what God has called us to do, every part of our spiritual life comes alive. There's a reason to grow. We have a compelling reason to pray, to stay in close contact with our Leader and Guide when we walk unfamiliar, threatening paths. There's a strong drive for fellowship, allies, and friends close at hand because what God calls us to, we can't do alone. There's an undeniable need for worship, a clear vision of who God is and His commitment to meet our every need as we walk with Him into the future.

Dreams make us aware of resources. We discover resources we may not have known we had. With so much information bombarding our minds through our five senses, our brain has a built-in system that filters out information that is not pertinent to us. Anyone who has ever bought a car has seen this principle in operation. We go to a car dealer, pick out and buy a car, and drive away thinking our car is a new "unique"-color — only to begin to notice that many other cars have this "unique" color.

The fact is, until we identify a dream, we will probably not notice many of the resources God has laid right at our feet. Many people assume that their dreams are impossible because what is needed is not available, when in fact the resources were there all along. They just didn't notice (or need) them.

Dreams lead us to discover previously unrecognized potential God built into our design. We'll discover spiritual, physical, emotional, or intellectual muscles we never knew we had. Many of our former college classmates are shocked that Kathy is a best-selling author, given her less-than-studious reputation as a student. As she puts it, she majored in social science—heavy on the social, light on the science. Her skill and success at writing surprised her as much as anyone. She has discovered all kinds of God-given talents that lay dormant for years, until she began to dream.

> You can be sure that God will take care of everything you need, his generosity exceeding even yours in the glory that pours from Jesus.
>
> —PHILIPPIANS 4:19, MSG

> Although men are accused of not knowing their own weakness, yet perhaps a few know their own strength. It is in man as in soils, where sometimes there is a vein of gold which the owner knows not of.
>
> —JONATHAN SWIFT, ENGLISH WRITER

Dreams give us direction. Our dreams may not be impractical ideas we can't get out of our heads. They may be the sovereign hand of God guiding our decisions. Philippians mentions the inside-out workings of His Spirit. God not only opens the doors to fulfill our dreams, but He actually gives us the will to do what is necessary to fulfill His purpose. "For it is God who works in you to will and to act according to his good purpose" (Philippians 2:13).

Our eighteen-year-old son, Joel, has a dream—a big dream of someday winning the Masters golf tournament. His dream began the first time he ever picked up a golf club and hit the ball an amazing distance when he was fifteen. This dream drives him to practice every—and we mean *every*—spare minute he has left over after school and chores. His desire to improve his golf game affects his choices about other activities, where he'll go to college, and how he orders his day. We are trying to help him pursue this dream every way we can because we know how God has given him a will to pursue his dream and the talent to go along with it.

David speaks of the process of God's leading as follows:

> *I will instruct you and teach you in the way you*
> *should go;*
> *I will counsel you and watch over you. (Psalm 32:8)*

Dreams keep us on track. A dream acts like a default mechanism, giving us the ability to make consistent decisions in the direction of our dream even when we feel lost in the details. Cooperating with the Holy Spirit in the pursuit of a dream will keep us on course even when we can't see where we're going.

> There is no road to success but through a clear, strong purpose.

Anyone Can Dream

Grand dreams about new businesses, inventions, discoveries, missions, and ministries; ways to make our world a better place; and ways to make an impact on our culture are waiting to be conceived by ordinary people who have an extraordinary God—an extraordinary God who equips us to dream those dreams: "For God hath not given us the spirit of fear; but of power, and of love, and of a sound mind" (2 Timothy 1:7, KJV). Because God is infinite, all of the good ideas cannot possibly be exhausted. In fact, we believe that God has grand dreams for you to dream.

> Attempt great things for God; expect great things from God.
>
> —WILLIAM CAREY, MISSIONARY TO INDIA

Sadly, though, not everyone feels the freedom to dream. Some of us are living so fast and furiously today that we miss God's messages about tomorrow. Some believe that great things are only done by great men or women—and they don't feel a part of that elite group. For others, dreaming stopped in the second grade when they were reprimanded about daydreaming. Others still fear dreaming and, having tried it once and faced setbacks and rejections, felt as though they failed, and now they are determined never to travel in that far country again.

• •

God doesn't want us to be shy with his gifts, but bold and loving and sensible.

—2 Timothy 1:7

Anyone can, and probably should, dream, and any dream can be a dream from God. When we talk about God's work, we tend to think of Bible heroes or other historic or contemporary figures who do capital-*B* big things. In reality, our dreams—and what we do with them, as we shall see—affect all parts of our lives. A dream doesn't have to be about an invention, a miracle, a cure for cancer, an end to war. It doesn't have to be about starting a multimillion-dollar business or making a blockbuster movie. Sometimes the "smallest" of dreams are the most profound. Children, spouses, family, friends, financial security, one's relationship with God—all these can be the subjects for our dreams.

Here are some questions for dreams about these "smaller" facets of life:

➠ If your family were operating at peak performance, what would it look like?

➠ Do you have a loving, intimate relationship with your spouse? How could you make your marriage better?

➠ Are you the parent you really want to be? Do you have a nurturing relationship with each of your children?

➠ Do you have friendships that support and encourage you? Describe your ideal best friend. continued on next page continued from previous page

➤ Are you comfortable financially? What could make you feel more secure?

➤ Are you satisfied with the community where you live? How could it be better?

➤ What products or services would you like to "take on" because you know you could make something or do something better?

➤ What supposedly impractical things have you always wanted to do but felt you couldn't? Are there legitimate reasons holding you back?

➤ What would you like your relationship with God to be? What difference would that make in your daily life?

CHAPTER

The Dawning of a Dream

Most people go to the grave with their music still inside them.

OLIVER WENDELL HOLMES

Sometimes I've believed as many as six impossible things before breakfast.

LEWIS CARROLL

April 14, 1961, is not a day most historians remember, but it was every bit as important as July 20, 1969, the day Neil Armstrong stepped into history as the first man on the moon. Those two dates mark the bookends of the most dramatic peacetime scientific endeavor in history. Make no mistake, the beginning was just as important as the realization.

That evening in 1961, John Kennedy gathered a handful of advisors at the White House. Kennedy seemed distracted and showed minimal interest as aerospace experts explained a ten-year, forty-billion-dollar program that had no guarantee of success. What no one else could see was that the dream factory in Kennedy's mind was operating at capacity. As Kennedy pondered facts he didn't fully understand and thought about a dream he feared he might never see become reality, something happened inside of him. Fifteen minutes after the meeting he gave the word: "We're going to the moon." How did that dream awaken inside Kennedy? *Time* magazine correspondent Hugh Sidey reflected on that day and gives us some insight.

> *This was not a military imperative. There was no overwhelming clamor from the public or Congress for such effort. Something special happened in the mind of Kennedy. The poet in him glimpsed the future, perhaps, the Irish combativeness responded to the prospects of a race. What we do know is that John Kennedy finally decided, in those few minutes, to take the nation on a peaceful and creative journey, the likes of which the world has never known.*[1]

Not all dreams from God make it into the history books like this one did. But every dream from God starts somewhere. The question is where. How does God awaken inside us the specific dreams He wants us to pursue? When we read stories like Kennedy's it seems so mystical—as if "poof," it just happened. Does a dream just appear out of the blue when we least expect it? Or is there something we do to engage the process? Those are the questions we will address in this chapter.

To be sure, there is a part of the dreaming process, when heaven touches earth, that defies knowledge and description. And, yes, sometimes dreams just seem to hit us, out of the blue. But what looks a lot like moon-

> People seldom see the halting and painful steps by which the most insignificant success is achieved.
>
> —ANN SULLIVAN,
> HELEN KELLER'S TEACHER

beams and magic to the casual observer is anything but effortless to the dreamer. Dreaming, more often than not, is accompanied by agonizing mental and emotional effort before it surfaces and declares, "We're going to the moon." The process, not so obvious in Kennedy's case, is laid bare for us in Nehemiah's life. We've looked at some of the elements already, and now we'll see how they form a mosaic of our part in preparing for the dawning of a dream.

Awaking to God's Dream

Twenty-five hundred years ago, Nehemiah's deep, heartfelt passion was transformed by God into a vision of the future. With an ever-distinguishing shape, his passion became a dream. We can observe and learn from parts of this process the crucial matter of allowing God's dream to dawn on us.

He was intent on his passion. The situation in Jerusalem was the focus of his life and his heart—not just for a day or a week, but for three or four months of anguished mental, emotional, and spiritual effort. It's likely there were many times Nehemiah would have loved to erase Jerusalem from his thoughts, yet it seemed as though God continually brought it to his mind. As Kathy says, it was one of those "beach ball" issues. Try to push it beneath the surface and it pops back up; you just can't keep it down. When Nehemiah opened his eyes in the morning, his mind raced to Jerusalem. As he performed his daily duties, he found it hard to concentrate. When he closed his eyes at night, he saw the misery of the people. Notice that he didn't run from this haunting vision. He embraced it, along with all its pain. As Nehemiah focused on his passion, something began to happen inside him, changing his behavior in noticeable ways.

He was realistic about the situation. Nehemiah was no idle daydreamer. As he dreamed about the changes that needed to be made in Jerusalem, he evaluated the situation realistically. Restoration of the walls was no small problem, even with today's engineering technology, which he most certainly did not have. Nehemiah faced real, not imagined, obstacles to his dream. The logistical nightmare, an unpredictable labor force in Jerusalem, a materials acquisition dilemma, a volatile political predicament—all these things loomed in his mind. Beyond those problems, Nehemiah was returning to a people who had been demoralized and defeated, left with very little sense of identity. They were ignorant of their spiritual resources, vulnerable to their neighbors, and totally preoccupied with survival.

Awaking to a dream from God is certainly not a matter of wishful thinking. The mind that dreams for God has its anchor in the reality of the situation. But that's not the only reality.

He was realistic about God. There was one thing that kept Nehemiah optimistic while being realistic: the size of his God. Compared to the size of the problem, the greatness of his God brought the problem into perspective.

> What comes to mind when we think of God is the most important thing about us.
>
> —A. W. Tozer

Researchers of human behavior have long recognized that there are two elements to a crisis: an individual's evaluation of the risk factor and his or her estimation of available resources to meet the challenge. The reason Nehemiah could face so huge a challenge was that he knew he had a God bigger than the problem. Nehemiah's God was "great and awesome." Not only that, He was absolutely committed to His people.

What comes to mind when we think of God will determine what we ask for. If He is harsh and exacting in our minds, we will plead and bargain for small favors. If He is stingy and uncaring, we won't ask at all. But if we see God as generous and gracious, we will come to Him with everything that burdens our heart.

He prayed. Nehemiah took his problem to the One who could do something about it. It's that simple. He had a conversation with his loving heavenly Father about the subject of his choice: his passion over the state of Jerusalem. He didn't use fancy words or employ special methods. He simply prayed.

We don't know how long this process took, but as Nehemiah pondered the situation and prayed, his passion for God's people and God's city began to crystallize in his mind and form an idea. As he continued to pray, he saw that perhaps he was the answer to his own prayer. Passion in prayer gave birth to a dream, and Nehemiah knew *he* had to do something.

• •

Our research consistently reveals that people in America want to make a difference in the world. For all their selfish tendencies and inward-looking practices, they want their life to count for something of lasting value. The means to that end is loving and serving God. The surest avenue to effectively growing that relationship is to capture His vision and live it to the fullest.

—GEORGE BARNA, AMERICAN FUTURIST

Turning Passions into Dreams

A dream, any dream, as we've said before, doesn't happen overnight. And every dream needs to begin somewhere. Before we can turn our dreams into reality, we need to awaken to the things that God wants to accomplish through us. How?

1. Continue to focus on the situation. Focusing means thinking about, praying about, and waiting for the right action to present itself. What seems to be the right course of action at first might not be. Give God a chance. As you focus on this heartfelt passion, something will begin to happen inside you. It will change who you are from the inside out, calling you to do something.

2. Search the Scripture. God has not revealed the totality of His

Growth Op

Visualize a need or opportunity you feel very strongly about. What would you love to see happen? Let your mind paint a picture of what would happen—best-case scenario.

specific will in the Scripture, but if there is a promise to claim, a command to obey, or an action to take in a given situation, Scripture can let us know if we're on target.

Even though the promises God made to Moses that Nehemiah referred to in his prayer didn't include the restoration of Jerusalem, Deuteronomy 28–30 gave him every reason to hope that it was God's will that His city should be in better shape than it was.

One thing's for sure, God will never lead us to violate His Word to fulfill a dream. We've either got the wrong dream or the wrong method. God's Word must always be the objective standard by which we evaluate our dreams.

Growth Op

Read a portion of the Bible every day. Keep a log recording the insights God gives you. Is there a promise to claim? A sin to avoid? An attribute of God to cling to? A blessing to thank Him for?

3. Expect the outrageous. Great dreams begin with ordinary ideas that pop into our minds. We never know when an idea may be valuable, no matter how outrageous. Rarely is the potential of an idea seen at first glance.

The first time Nehemiah thought to himself, *Well, maybe I can go to Jerusalem,* it's likely he dismissed it as a ludicrous idea. If we habitually dismiss outrageous thoughts, we'll miss God's voice at some point.

4. Hitchhike on ideas. A good reason to allow outrageous ideas to run loose in your mind is that they will lead to other ideas. Ideas build on each other as our minds race from one thought to the next. Think of thoughts as stairs; each one takes us closer to the idea we will pursue.

Growth Op

Take your mind out of the edit mode. What crazy ideas have you dismissed lately? Why?

5. Be realistic about the situation. Sometimes it's hard to be positive about life and realistic at the same time. We can think idealistically and be pretty positive—you know, bad things don't happen to good people, Christians don't have problems, believers don't go bankrupt, real disciples don't get depressed, and the ministers of the gospel don't have moral failures. If this is our view of life, we're not living in the real world and we'd better get ready because one day our bubble will burst. On the other hand, the problem with being realistic is that it leads us to think like Murphy, the guy with the law: If anything can go wrong, it will. If we believe that, we'll never dream, never take a chance, and ultimately lead a life of despair. The only way to be realistic and positive at the same time is to keep our situation and God in clear view at all times.

6. Remind yourself how big God is. As our kids would say, "It's all about perspective." How we see God determines how we see life. And it definitely determines how we look at our dreams. It's interesting to look at the story of Joshua, Caleb, and the ten spies Moses sent to spy out the Promised Land. Their response gives us a picture of how important it is to know how big God is. All twelve of these men saw the same land, the same blessings, the same fortifications, and the same people (big people—giants!). None of them underestimated the size of the task, nor did they overestimate it. But the ten spies certainly underestimated the size of their God (Numbers 13:28-33, 14:6-9).

7. Take it to God. As we pray, God will begin to retool our personality and change our behavior in a noticeable way until a dream is born within us that calls us and drives us with a sense of purpose we may have never felt before. As we continue to pray, at some point something about our passion will begin to crystallize in our mind. That's when we reach the point of becoming committed to making something happen. God's dream has dawned within us.

Make a list. What is the reality of your situation? What stands in the way? What makes you want to turn tail and run from your dream?

Make another list. Who is your God? Compare the obstacles you face with size of your God.

Undamming the River

In many ways a dream *is* like a river. It has incredible force and potential to make a difference in our lives—and in the world. But, also, like a river, it can become dammed up. Often people ask us, "What if I don't dream about anything? Is there something wrong with me?" Sad but true, many of us have dwelt in the land of the monotonous impossible so long that we've lost touch with the reality of the possible. We may need to relearn how to dream, following Nehemiah's example. But several barriers can thwart our efforts to relearn the dreaming process.

> We need to find God, and he cannot be found in noise and restlessness. God is the friend of silence. See how nature—trees, flowers, grass—grows in silence; see the stars, the moon and the sun, how they move in silence. . . . We need silence to be able to touch souls.
>
> —MOTHER TERESA

We're too busy. If our calendars are booked till eternity, if we never take time to stop and think, if we're always servicing interruptions and distractions that call for more attention than they deserve, we'll very likely never get in touch with the dreams God has planted within us.

There's an old adage that if you want to get something done, ask a busy person. And to a certain extent, that's true. Dreamers aren't only dreamers. As we shall see in the coming chapters, they are people who know how to implement plans to get things done. On the other hand, a person can implement all the plans in the world, but without a solid dream behind them, not much of lasting benefit is likely to happen. (To some, this is known as running around in circles.)

We have a friend who by her own admission and our knowledge of her, does get a lot done. She's self-employed, edits books, writes books, and goes to school full time. She does a lot of volunteer work for various community groups, and, as a single parent whose nest is empty, she makes sure to include some social time with friends in her busy schedule. She's also, as many of us are, in middle age, in the process of reevaluating her life to decide what God is calling her to do next. This all sounds pretty good on paper. The problem is, she is so busy keeping up with her daily commitments that, despite her heartfelt desire to focus on a dream and make some changes in her life, she can't ever seem to get around to it. She goes from idea to idea—they all sound good—and never takes the time to wait on God.

> One half of knowing what you want is knowing what you must give up before you get it.
>
> —SIDNEY HOWARD, AMERICAN PLAY-WRIGHT, PULITZER PRIZE WINNER

We're tired. Vince Lombardi was right when he said, "Fatigue makes cowards of us all." If we're drained, depressed, and just plain tired, chances are we won't be able to dream. Dreaming takes energy. If we don't take time to take care of ourselves, if we don't schedule times of rest and refreshment into our lives, we rob ourselves of the energy we need to be able to dream.

> Life develops from within.
>
> —ELIZABETH BARRETT BROWNING

We've forgotten how to enjoy life. Strange as it seems, laughter and fun are dream enhancers. But it's easy for our lives to become out of balance, weighted down by all work and little or no play—not an environment conducive for dreaming. Even though we are about serious tasks, fun needs to be built into every day. Norman Cousins reported in *Anatomy of an Illness* that joyful laughter causes the brain to create endorphins, which relieve stress, activate the immune system, and seem to be linked to energy renewal.

> He who laughs, lasts.
>
> —ANONYMOUS

We're disconnected. Attempting to connect with others even when we're in despair is a good balance to the alone time we need to hatch a dream. Other dreamers can provide invaluable services: they can add to our dreams or we to theirs. They can provide feedback that keeps us grounded in reality.

> As iron sharpens iron,
>   so one man sharpens another.
>
> —PROVERBS 27:17

We fear failure. When we experience failure, it's easy to think, *I'll never dream again. That was too risky. It hurt too much to fail.* Oftentimes we stop dreaming at the very point when things are about to happen.

• •

Far better it is to dare mighty things, to win glorious triumphs, even though checkered by failure, than to take rank with those poor spirits who neither enjoy much nor suffer much, because they live in the gray twilight that knows not victory nor defeat.

—Theodore Roosevelt

Fear of any sort, especially of failure, can give us a myopic view of life. Our sense of reality gets shaky. Our world shrinks. If our small world does not include God (and most of the time it seems it doesn't), then fear and despair will prevail in our lives. We'll feel trapped and unable to do anything about the circumstances around us.

We fear criticism. Criticism, valid or not, can hurt so much it tempts us to stop dreaming. Remember the elephant from chapter 1? Repeated criticism can stop our dreams as surely as that two-foot stake of limitations—if we let it.

We also fear rejection. God never said to Moses or to Nehemiah or to Mary, the mother of Jesus, or to any of Jesus' disciples that they would be loved and held in high esteem by their peers. In fact, if we dream only dreams that guarantee we won't be rejected (or criticized) by someone, we're probably not dreaming big enough. The reality is, the world is not always an especially friendly place for dreamers.

It's only when we begin to see a reality larger than ourselves and our present situation that we will realize that there is a God who is able to move past our pain and fear—and use it for good—into a larger reality. Many times He uses failure and pain to move us to the place where we will call on Him, because He has been waiting all along to answer.

You are forgiving and good, O LORD,
  abounding in love to all who call to you.
Hear my prayer, O LORD;
  listen to my cry for mercy.
In the day of my trouble I will call to you,
  for you will answer me. (Psalm 86:5-7)

Growth Op

What's damming your river? Do you need to schedule some time away from the noise of life so that you can hear God's voice clearly? Read and meditate on the following verses.

Call to me and I will answer you and tell you great and unsearchable things you do not know. (Jeremiah 33:3)

Be strong and courageous. Do not be terrified; do not be discouraged, for the LORD your God will be with you wherever you go. (Joshua 1:9)

Surely the arm of the LORD is not too short to save, nor his ear too dull to hear. (Isaiah 59:1)

9

How to Spot a Dream from God

*The devil hath power to assume
a pleasing shape.*

WILLIAM SHAKESPEARE

By now, there shouldn't be much question about the value of dreams. But in dreams, as with everything else in life, not everything is of equal value. Earlier in the book we talked about sin. Sometimes it's easy to spot which dreams spring from our own selfishness and which spring from the deep call of God. Sometimes, however, Satan puts a spin on a dream that can make even evil look beautiful.

Just because we have a dream doesn't mean we should pursue it. Some dreams are inherently sinful and obviously not from God, like lustfully dreaming about someone else's car, house, or job. The Bible calls that coveting.

Some dreams aren't inherently sinful, but the cost of pursuing them might be. I think back to the time I published my first book. What if we didn't have two thousand dollars in savings to use? What if pursuing my dream would have meant not having money for the house payment or food for our children? Had that been the case, I might have been led to see that either I needed to pursue my dream in a different way or that it wasn't, after all, a dream from God—or not His timing.

Even good dreams can have bad foundations. A dream about a new business can be dominated by greed or pride rather than seen as a vehicle for providing a quality service, a product, or employment for others. We can dream about being elected to an influential position at the expense of someone else's reputation or because of a lust for power. We can pervert any of God's blessings. Satan is at work helping us do just that, and he is very intense in such matters, as the apostle Peter tells us: "Be sober, be vigilant; because your adversary the devil, as a roaring lion, walketh about, seeking whom he may devour" (1 Peter 5:8, KJV).

Adolph Hitler had a dream—the dream of a pure human race. The Unabomber had a dream of a simpler society. A friend of ours had a dream for a fulfilling marriage—to his nurse rather than his wife. Dreams that are harmful to others, destructive and sinful, need to be recognized for their origin, labeled for what they are, and dismissed from our minds. The apostle Paul provides us an excellent set of standards to evaluate our dreams by: "Finally, brothers, whatever is true, whatever is noble, whatever is right, whatever is pure, whatever is lovely, whatever is admirable—if anything is excellent or praiseworthy—think about such things" (Philippians 4:8).

Dreaming is unfamiliar ground to many of us, and sometimes that makes us unduly skeptical. We distrust our desires. We lack the faith to believe God places dreams within us. We rationalize our longings and pack them away neatly in the back of our mind. We don't trust ourselves to know whether a dream is really from God.

If the very act of dreaming can make us skeptical, and if even good dreams can have bad foundations, how can we tell the difference between a dream from our own ego or Satan and a dream from God? I think the only way is by asking hard questions at the beginning and throughout the dreaming process. We've discovered seven questions that help discern the crucial matter of whether or not a dream is from God.

> Be self-controlled and alert. Your enemy the devil prowls around like a roaring lion looking for someone to devour.
>
> —1 Peter 5:8

> A good question to ask about any dream is, Can this be done for the glory of God?

> There isn't a person anywhere who isn't capable of doing more than he thinks he can.
>
> —Henry Ford

Does the Dream Push My Envelope?

God's dreams stretch us. They cause us to reach for things we thought we could never experience, to risk what we thought we could never lose, to hope for what we thought we could never gain. Dreams cause us to tap into potential energy, discover resources we thought we didn't have. They demand that we develop a stronger, deeper, more significant relationship with God than we've ever had before, to embrace the impossible and believe it's possible because we worship the God of the impossible.

A dream from God lays hold of the "good works" that we were created for in Jesus Christ. His dreams bring our innermost being meaning and purpose as we've never experienced before. When we put ourselves in God's hands, He will simply not allow us to stay comfortably complacent in our own small worlds.

God's dreams are often outrageous and extravagant. They press the envelope of what most people would consider probable. God's dreams demand more energy, more time, more resources than we can possibly muster on our own. If our first thought is, *This will be a piece of cake; I can do this without help*, then perhaps it's not God's dream.

> A great wind is blowing, and that gives you either imagination or a headache.
>
> —CATHERINE II, EMPRESS OF RUSSIA (1729–1796)

Does My Dream Embrace Change?

Change is healthy for any person, animal, organism, or organization. To embrace the status quo almost always ensures death. Nothing can ever stay the same. It will either grow or die. Such is life.

A dream from God goes beyond just accepting change as inevitable. It actually celebrates and rejoices in the possibility of change. God is a God of creativity and diversity and is constantly pushing His creatures to move toward the ideal of what He created them to be, to be conformed into the image of Jesus Christ.

Change has been an inevitable part of our world, even before the Fall. When God commanded Adam and Eve to be fruitful and multiply, to fill the earth and subdue it, He was talking about more than having babies and commanding the animals.

> Change is the law of life. And those who look only to the past or present are certain to miss the future.
>
> —JOHN F. KENNEDY

Part of the creation mandate is to create a culture and develop the world into all that God created it to be.

Creation, as God designed it, demands change. If you consider the Fall and the desperate situation that our world has been cast into, the need for change becomes even more compelling. To accept the status quo is to accept Satan's domination of the earth. It is to refuse to dream about the day that all creation longs for when creation will be redeemed. Paul writes about this in Romans:

> *The creation waits in eager expectation for the sons of God to be revealed. For the creation was subjected to frustration, not by its own choice, but by the will of the one who subjected it, in hope that the creation itself will be liberated from its bondage to decay and brought into the glorious freedom of the children of God.*
>
> *We know that the whole creation has been groaning as in the pains of childbirth right up to the present time.* (Romans 8:19-22)

Is My Dream People-Focused?

God's vision ultimately focuses on changing people, not building buildings, selling widgets, or creating programs. Those things are always a means to an end. Examine Nehemiah's dream to rebuild the walls of Jerusalem, and you will quickly see that his purpose was to bring glory to God and to restore the people in the nation of Israel. God's dreams pull you out of selfishness and preoccupation with your greed to something bigger than yourself.

Do all the good you can,
By all the means you can,
In all the ways you can,
In all the places you can,
At all the times you can,
To all the people you can,
As long as ever you can.

—JOHN WESLEY

No matter where God's dream focuses—bettering our family, developing real estate, starting a ministry, opening a store—the dreams that come from God have to do with empowering people and meeting legitimate spiritual, emotional, and physical needs, ultimately serving God in the process.

Tom Peters, author and marketing consultant, says businesses that aren't people-oriented will be out of business shortly. All dreams have to do with resources of one form or another, but the focus must always be on people.

Does My Dream Use My Unique Gifts and Talents?

> If a man does not keep pace with his companions, perhaps it is because he hears a different drummer. Let him step to the music which he hears, however measured or far away.
>
> —HENRY DAVID THOREAU

Each of us listens to a different drummer or, more precisely, a different drumbeat, because each of us is designed to pursue a unique calling. God has specific things in mind for you and only you, and He will put His dreams in your heart to move you toward those specific things.

It's fascinating to ponder that never before in the history of the world has there ever been a person just like you, nor will there ever be. You are a one-of-a-kind masterpiece, and no one else can fulfill the purpose for which you were created, or even *tell* you the purpose for which you were created. Other people can affirm you, give you input and guidance, encourage or discourage you, but you simply can't get your dreams from pals, heroes, Mom and Dad, your pastor, a colleague, or anyone else. Only you can dream the dream that God created for you and only you can fulfill that dream.

> The place where God calls you to is the place where your deep gladness and the world's deep hunger meet.
>
> —FREDERICK BUECHNER, AMERICAN THEOLOGIAN

A dream from God allows us to lay hold of the specifics of our individual destiny. Because God's dreams call for us to believe great things, they call forth the best in us.

114

Does the Dream Awaken My Emotions?

Dreams from God are not something you can be neutral about. They evoke strong feelings of passion, joy, anticipation, hope, and at times, anxiety.

To have great passion means to be willing to "bet the farm" on your dream. But dreams that are all passion and no wisdom serve no purpose other than to satisfy our own greed. Because the heart is deceitful above all things and desperately wicked (Jeremiah 17:9), we can desire and passionately move toward good dreams too quickly or rashly, or maybe when we shouldn't be moving at all. That's why it's important to weigh our emotions against the other criteria of a dream from God.

> Beware what you set your heart upon, for it surely shall be yours.
>
> —RALPH WALDO EMERSON

What Is the Cost?

Dreams can introduce another experience into our lives, one we don't like to think about: pain. Dreaming has a price. Sometimes a big price. By nature, dreaming moves us out of our comfort zone where life is uneventful but seemingly safe. But that's not the life Jesus described to His disciples. When He outlined the cost of following Him, "many of his disciples turned back and no longer followed him" (John 6:66). Dreaming certainly brings a boat-load of benefits but more times than not there is a huge price to pay—and it usually comes before the payoff. Don't despair. That price is a good indication that what you dream about is from God. In fact if it cost too little maybe you aimed too low.

> He is no fool who gives what he cannot keep to gain that which he cannot lose.
>
> —JIM ELLIOT

It is, however, possible to pay too high a price. If I have to compromise my integrity, hurt someone else, or injure my relationship with God, the price is not right. No dream is worth that price.

Is My Dream Compelling?

Nothing great was ever achieved without enthusiasm.

—Ralph Waldo Emerson

God's dreams grip us and say, "Do something! Do something! Do something!" They bring strength out of fatigue and move us into action. They cause us to work late in the night and forget what time it is or work through a meal and forget we're hungry. If you find yourself working, working, working, and energized, that's probably a good sign.

The launching of Kathy's Family Manager project was a huge undertaking. For five months she managed our family and her company almost nonstop and got only five hours of sleep a night. When I reminded her that her body needed more rest, she agreed and slept a couple of extra hours for a few nights. But in no time, it seemed, she was at it again. Obviously, she couldn't live like that for long, but she had no problem giving 110 percent for a time to get off the ground what she believes to be a dream from God. Her dream compels and energizes her.

Growth Op

As you ponder your dreams and wonder whether they're really from God, ask yourself the questions in this chapter. Then as you pursue your dreams, come back and ask the questions again and again.

Question, Question, Question

Here's a checklist of questions we would do well to ask ourselves about each of our dreams. We need not necessarily be suspicious of our dreams, but rather very suspicious of our motives. Our motives are key in determining if the dream is indeed from God.

1. Why do I want to do this?
2. Am I doing this because I believe it's what God would have me do, or am I doing it for my own selfish desires?

3. If my dream came true, whose glory would be more important to me: mine or God's?
4. Will I be able to put God first in my life if I pursue this dream?
5. Will my dream affect other people?
6. Is this a good time for my dream to come to pass?
7. Would I be able to use my gifts and talents if I pursued this dream? Would the dream bring out the best in me?
8. Does my dream have confirmation from others?
9. Is this dream one that I should pursue myself, or am I to help someone else make it happen?
10. Is there something I should do today to move toward this dream?

10

Preparing for Your Journey

Don't wait for your ship to come in;
swim out to it.

ANONYMOUS

Always give yourselves fully
to the work of the Lord,
because you know that your labor
in the Lord is not in vain.

THE APOSTLE PAUL, 1 CORINTHIANS 15:58

"**B**e Prepared." It's the Boy Scout motto, and it's also the motto of an inveterate dreamer. And this characteristic is what separates the men from the boys—or the women from the girls, as the case may be.

Living with a radical dreamer can test the internal fortitude of anyone. I should know. I've shared the same bed and toothpaste with one for twenty-five years. Kathy Peel, a.k.a. Ms. You Never Know When Opportunity Will Knock, is always prepared for what's at hand and is invariably preparing for what the future could hold. As her husband, this is good news and bad news. It's bad news when we're going on a trip and I can't close the trunk of the car after stuffing in her suitcases. She thinks it's important to be prepared and pack a few "extra" items *just in case* the governor of the state we're driving through asks us to pop in for dinner, or we have an opportunity to attend an impromptu ball, high tea, golf tournament, or safari. She also packs enough medicine to treat every ailment known to humankind and enough food to get us through a month-long famine.

It's good news when it comes to her dreams. If you've ever run into her at an airport, you'll understand me perfectly when I say that she's always prepared as if her dreams were a reality. She's dressed to perfection—the reason being, she explains: "Who knows? Today might be the day my seat will be next to the head of ABC or the editor of *Time* magazine. I want to look my best and be prepared for a good interview." It makes sense to her. (I used to make fun of her until one day I was running through an airport in sloppy jeans and ran into the president of a publishing company. I wasn't at, or even close to, my "business best.") If Kathy has an idea for a book or a project but doesn't have a clue who might publish it, that doesn't stop her from gathering data and doing research. Every day she does something, even if it's just a little something, to move her in the direction of her dreams. I don't know about you, but I call that active faith. Some people would, no doubt, call it compulsive. But if a person has a dream he or she thinks is from

God and sits around waiting for the door of opportunity to open before doing anything, I call that unbelief. If a dream is from God, then the question is not *if* the door will open, but *when*. Don't get caught unprepared.

● ●

The secret of success in life is for a man to be ready for his opportunity when it comes.

—BENJAMIN DISRAELI, PRIME MINISTER OF GREAT BRITAIN (1804–1881)

When Dreams Become Opportunities

Sometimes doors of opportunity open slowly, even incrementally. Sometimes they don't open at all. And sometimes they swing wide open and an opportunity comes upon us with such unexpected speed it jolts our mind. This is what happened to Nehemiah. After three to four months of intense prayer and deep concern even to the point of, I suspect, giving up, almost without warning the hand of God moved swiftly and visibly into his life. Nehemiah describes the situation in detail for us.

> *In the month of Nisan in the twentieth year of King Artaxerxes, when wine was brought for him, I took the wine and gave it to the king. I had not been sad in his presence before; so the king asked me, "Why does your face look so sad when you are not ill? This can be nothing but sadness of heart."*
> *I was very much afraid. (Nehemiah 2:1-2)*

Nehemiah wrote about a private dinner for the king and queen. He was present, as usual, tasting the food and wine, putting his life on the line for the king. Nehemiah assures us that, so far, he had been able to conceal his preoccupation and despair over Jerusalem. But evidently his burden became too great to bear, and on this occasion the king noticed that something was wrong with his cupbearer.

One of the things you'd probably watch carefully, if you were an ancient Near Eastern king whose job description included being a potential assassination target, would be the face of the person who tasted your wine and sampled your food. On this particular night, when he saw Nehemiah's sad face, the king was understandably disturbed. It was actually against the law to grieve in the presence of the king. When the king saw Nehemiah, we can probably safely speculate that he suspected a plot against his life.

In that brief moment, the success or failure of all Nehemiah had prayed for hung in the balance. According to God's divine plan, the timing was right, the door had been opened—"Behold, I have set before thee an open door, and no man can shut it" (Revelation 3:8, KJV)—and Nehemiah had to explain himself. There was no way out. Either the king would respond positively and allow Nehemiah to move forward on his dream, or he would respond negatively and Nehemiah would lose his life. It was that simple.

Although the text does not state this, since Nehemiah was a regular human being like us he probably had second thoughts and longed to rethink what he was doing and control his unconscious display of grief. He had no intention of pressing this issue, but now he couldn't go back. What was done, was done.

• •

"I know you well; you aren't strong, but you have tried to obey and have not denied my Name. Therefore I have opened a door to you that no one can shut."

—REVELATION 3:8, TLB

Contemplating the possibilities, Nehemiah was understandably afraid. Very much afraid. It seems he had a number of options at this point, one of which would be to deny that anything was wrong, try to cover his tracks, and assure the king that nothing was going on. However, Nehemiah also knew that this might be the very time, the very occasion God had orchestrated for him to explain his desire to the king.

Nehemiah knew that his presence with King Artaxerxes was not the only royal audience he enjoyed at that moment. Having been continually in the presence of the King of kings for weeks, he had the courage to answer the earthly king.

> Life's great opportunities often open on the road of daily duties.
>
> —ANONYMOUS

> *I said to the king, "May the king live forever! Why should my face not look sad when the city where my fathers are buried lies in ruins, and its gates have been destroyed by fire?" (Nehemiah 2:3)*

Nehemiah's explanation was straightforward and incriminating. He was guilty of sadness of heart, but not for the reason the king had suspected. I imagine the moment between his response and the king's answer seemed like an eternity to Nehemiah. Finally, the king responded positively, "What is it you want?" (2:4).

Nehemiah recognized that this was the opportunity he had prayed and prepared for, and that God had opened the door. So he shot a quick prayer to God, and a request to the king:

> *Then I prayed to the God of heaven, and I answered the king, "If it pleases the king and if your servant has found favor in his sight, let him send me to the city in Judah where my fathers are buried so that I can rebuild it." (2:5)*

Nehemiah had active faith. Even though he was caught by surprise, he was not caught off guard. Those three to four months of waiting were not filled with idle wishes and day-

> I will study and get ready and the opportunity will come.
>
> —ABRAHAM LINCOLN

dreaming. He prayed fervently, planned diligently, and prepared faithfully. So when the door swung open, he was prayed up, planned up, and pumped up. He was ready to roll.

Getting Packed for the Journey

We must never forget that God is responsible for opening the door, but we must be ready to walk through it—if, that is, we want to turn our dreams into opportunities. Like Nehemiah, we must pray, plan, and prepare—but then we must persevere. Right now, the door to fulfilling your dream may be closed, locked, and shut tighter than a vault. But this may be the time to acknowledge that nothing is standing in the way of that door opening—except your own faith and commitment. It may be time to prepare.

If you've got a dream within you that you believe is from God, now is the time to move on it. Today, not tomorrow. *But*, perhaps you're thinking, *I can't just up and quit my job, or move across the country, or go to the bank and get a loan for my idea.* Okay. It might be too soon to make drastic moves. Maybe God hasn't opened the right doors just yet. It takes time to get dreams in place. But there are some things you can always do to prepare in case the door should open.

> When Noah built the ark, it wasn't raining yet.

Preparing Spiritually for the Journey

Through a process we believe by faith but do not completely understand, God is at work in our lives. In Philippians 1:6 Paul writes, "He who began a good work in you will carry it on to completion until the day of Christ Jesus." As I regularly spend time with God through prayer, reading and studying His Word, trying to practice His presence, and striving to obey His principles, He transforms me into the person He created me to be to fulfill the purpose for which He created me.

As we gradually grow in our relationship to God, we discover new understanding about who we are and what we are to do. We receive strength—strength to wait with patience, to endure hard circumstances, and to desire God's will instead of ours.

Being prepared spiritually is the single most important thing we can do to ensure that our dreams come true. In fact, preparing spiritually for a dream is no different from living out a life of faith. And that's the point. We believe one of the requirements of living in faith is preparing to dream God's dreams and working to bring them to fruition. You might even say we have the responsibility to dream.

Slowly but surely, as we get to know God in a deeper way, we learn that we can trust Him more. We have more courage to step out on the dreams we think are from Him. Getting to know Him also allows us to relax and to give thanks in more and more situations, and to accept with joyous gratitude the way He created us and the circumstances in which He places us.

We need perspective. Large doses of perspective. Knowing God in a deeper way gives me perspective when I'm frantically running around trying to open doors by myself and manipulate situations and people, trying to make my dreams come true in my own way, on my own timetable. Perspective helps me remember that I'm responsible for developing my relationship with God — getting to know Him better and better each day. If I do that, He'll take care of my dreams — preparing the way, opening the doors, working behind the scenes to put the pieces together. He takes care of the where, when, and how much better than I ever could.

None of us can grow deeper in relationship to God, though, without devoting time to it. And when we do take time to develop our spiritual life, other things — our dreams, plans, circumstances — start taking care of themselves. We know what we're supposed to do, and miraculously, we have time, resources, and energy to do it.

> "Seek first his [your heavenly Father's] kingdom and his righteousness, and all these things will be given to you as well."
>
> —Matthew 6:33

To prepare ourselves for our journey spiritually, we need to develop a relationship with God. I'm not referring to some special emotion or tingle down our spine. Nor am I talking about hearing voices or seeing visions. God is a person, and He can be known as a person in the same way a son knows his father, a wife knows her husband, or a friend knows a friend—relationships the Bible uses as analogies for our relationship with God. The Scripture also shows us six facets about getting to know God.

1. Knowing God begins with reconciliation. The prerequisite to a relationship with God is dealing with sin. The fact is, no one can approach God and hope to know Him while still in rebellion. Fortunately, God made the first move to end our rebellion by sending Christ. Paul says,

> *For if, when we were God's enemies, we were reconciled to him through the death of his Son, how much more, having been reconciled, shall we be saved through his life! Not only is this so, but we also rejoice in God through our Lord Jesus Christ, through whom we have now received reconciliation. (Romans 5:10-11)*

Our relationship with God is established through Christ. Through Him, our sin, which was a barrier, is removed and our place in God's family is secured. Once this initial barrier is cleared, we come to know God as we do any other person.

2. Knowing God takes time. It's a universal rule: If it's valuable, it takes time. Only as I spend time with another person do I come to know her, see what she sees, learn what she likes and dislikes, understand how she responds in a crisis. There is no knowing, no growing, without time.

It's not strange that we should want to spend time with God, but it is amazing that He wants to spend time with us. Mark 3:14 is one of the most remarkable verses in the Bible because it reveals this desire of God: "He appointed twelve—designating them apostles—that they might be with him and that he might send them out to preach."

Imagine! The Sovereign Creator of the universe wants to "be" with me, and He wants me to be with Him!

3. Knowing God demands communication. Communication has two elements: listening and talking. As with most of our relationships, we should listen a lot more than we talk. We listen to God speak through

His Word. The books of the Bible are more than a dusty set of ancient manuscripts. They are the living Word of God.

For the word of God is living and active. Sharper than any double-edged sword, it penetrates even to dividing soul and spirit, joints and marrow; it judges the thoughts and attitudes of the heart. (Hebrews 4:12)

Every time we pick up the Bible, it's as if God speaks afresh to us. In His Word He tells us what He is like, what He promises, and how He wants us to live. Listen to how Paul says it: "All Scripture is God-breathed and is useful for teaching, rebuking, correcting and training in righteousness, so that the man of God may be thoroughly equipped for every good work" (2 Timothy 3:16-17).

As we grow in our knowledge of God, we learn to listen to Him speak to us in our thoughts and recognize His voice. It's as if we're thinking His thoughts. A friend of ours explained this principle beautifully.

When her husband's company transferred him to Italy, Diane knew it would be important to learn the language. She enrolled in Italian classes and studied diligently. After two semesters, although she had learned a lot of vocabulary words and understood sentence structure and pronunciation, she was disappointed because she still couldn't speak the language. She continued to study, read books in the language, and listen to tapes. Finally, one day as she was walking in an open-air market, something happened. She began *thinking* in Italian. All of her studying and getting the language inside her had paid off. She was now bilingual.

In a way, that's what happens when we get God's Word inside of us. We become bilingual. We begin to think in "God's language."

Communication also involves speaking. Our conversation should be characterized by honest words and honest praise. Open acknowledgment of our desires and feelings before God is essential for intimacy. Over and over in the Psalms we read of how David poured his heart out honestly to God. We are to do the same.

4. Knowing God takes commitment. Commitment is the foundation for any relationship. Without commitment, communication will remain shallow and relationships will be superficial. When we reveal ourselves to someone else, we become vulnerable. In every deep and intimate relationship there is mutual commitment. We know God's level of commitment from His Word: "He who did not spare his own Son, but gave him up for us all—how will he not also, along with him, graciously give us all things?" (Romans 8:32).

God's commitment to us is undeserved, unconditional, and total. He holds nothing back. Although His love is not dependent on our response, He asks us to respond with that same level of commitment. As we commit ourselves to Him, He is able to open more of Himself up to us.

> *Therefore, I urge you, brothers, in view of God's mercy, to offer your bodies as living sacrifices, holy and pleasing to God—this is your spiritual [or reasonable] act of worship. Do not conform any longer to the pattern of this world, but be transformed by the renewing of your mind. Then you will be able to test and approve what God's will is—his good, pleasing and perfect will. (Romans 12:1-2)*

No one will make that kind of commitment to a contrived image of God. But because of who God is and what He has done, Paul calls this a reasonable act of worship. As I open myself to God, He reveals Himself more and more intimately to me. It is impossible to know God intimately without having an obedient heart.

5. Knowing God demands risk. Unfortunately, it's all too easy to accumulate fascinating facts about God without coming face-to-face with Him. We can know all about Him theoretically without really knowing Him experientially. Knowledge about who God is only becomes knowledge of God Himself when we step out and put what we have been told on the line of reality. We won't know the Lord is good until we "taste and see" for ourselves, as He invites us to do in Psalm 34:8. We won't know that God is faithful until we act as if He is present, even when it seems He has walked off the job. We won't know that God accepts us totally by grace and on the merits of Christ alone until we come expecting Him to bless us even though we know we are unworthy. We won't know Christ and that what He gives us is all we need until we relinquish our demands for others to love us and learn to rest in His love alone.

6. Knowing God is a matter of grace. Lest we forget, let's remind ourselves that God is the initiator of intimacy. If He did not want to be known, we would never know Him. Incredibly, God pursues us into the pits of humanity and shines the knowledge of Himself into our dark world. Jesus told the woman at the well, "Yet a time is coming and has now come when the true worshipers will worship the Father in spirit and truth, for they are the kind of worshipers the Father seeks" (John 4:23).

God is not seeking men and women who want to make their own gods—whether in their minds or at their workshops. He is looking for men and women who are desperate for real answers, real life, and knowledge of the real God.

Growth Op

There's no time like the present, as the saying goes. Start today. Tell God about your dream. Listen to His response through Scripture and quiet waiting. Acknowledge your own faults and needs, and make a commitment to spend some time with God—today and every day. This is the way to prepare for the journey of fulfilling your dream.

• •

One of life's most painful moments comes when we must admit that we didn't do our homework, that we are not prepared.

—MERLIN OLSEN, FORMER NFL PLAYER

Preparing Mentally for the Journey

Perhaps you'll relate to our son, who, as a high schooler, began to grow in his knowledge of God. When he learned that God would meet all his needs, he announced to us one night that he would rather spend time with his friends the night before a big test than pore over his chemistry book. Surely God would supply the needed answers.

We explained to him that God does meet all our needs. But one way God meets our need to know chemistry or any other subject is by giving us the ability and resources to learn what we need to learn. When we have a dream, it's our job to do the groundwork, to hit the books, to acquire the knowledge and skills we need to turn the dream into a reality.

Divine whiffle dust. That's what many people want when it comes to turning a dream into an opportunity. They don't understand that dreams require diligence, hard work, and tenacity. It's at this point that a dream either remains just a dream or moves toward becoming a reality.

If you have a compelling dream from God, you'll find it hard to sit in your recliner in front of the television night after night. Instead, you'll find yourself thinking, researching, and writing down ideas, information, numbers, or names. You'll ponder steps you need to take and people you need to talk with. You'll think through the logistics, the ramifications, the implications. You'll begin mentally preparing yourself to be the best you can be to fulfill your dream.

When the door opened for Nehemiah, he was mentally prepared. He knew exactly what he needed to get the job done, and for such a massive undertaking, he must have burned a lot of midnight oil.

Let's flesh out this mental preparation for the journey of fulfilling your dream. What does it entail?

1. Preparing mentally begins with research. When Kathy began to dream about creating Family Manager resources to help busy women run their homes more efficiently, she researched and prepared for three years. She spent a lot of time, energy, and money before God finally opened the door. Many days it seemed like she was working for nothing and that all her research and preparation would go down the tube. Her belief that God had planted the idea in her kept her going.

2. Preparing mentally requires training. One of the most frustrating things she had to learn when she started writing was to use a computer. Since she didn't want to handwrite manuscripts the rest of her life, she thought this was well worthwhile, even though she hated having to learn all the new computer language. Today, when she has four or five magazine articles and a book due the same week, she's glad she's computer-literate. When I took a new job that included producing a newsletter, I took a course on newsletter design. I still use the skills I learned in that course every time I communicate on paper with people.

3. Preparing mentally means cultivating relationships with mentors and teachers. God has not only given us Himself, He's given us people.

I wasn't too far into my speaking career before I realized I needed help. I had spoken at some small events, but before I moved to bigger audiences I felt I needed some professional guidance. I read books on how to be a better speaker, listened to tapes, and watched polished speakers on television. But what I really needed was the help of an expert. Through a friend's recommendation, I went to a speaking coach who critiqued my style and helped me immensely. When the first big invitation came, I felt like I had done all I could to prepare myself for the job. Then it was up to God.

> Any two of us are smarter than any one of us.
>
> —WAYNE PAULSON

4. Preparing mentally means being open to learning opportunities. Learning requires hunger. A mentally hungry person is always looking for opportunities to learn something new. This involves not just hanging around the library or bookstore but learning from what happens to us daily. It's like being a perpetual student, or as my dad says, a lifelong learner.

> I think that knowing what you do not know is more important than knowing what you know.
>
> —LUCILLE BALL

Learning requires humility. We can't figure out what we need to know until we're ready to admit what we don't know. And sometimes what we need to know comes wrapped in very strange packages. And sometimes our teachers are not the ones we would choose.

> The greatest lesson in life is to know that even fools can be right sometimes.
>
> —WINSTON CHURCHILL

131

Growth Op

From whom have you learned lately? Your children? Your parents? Your critics? Your enemies? Your pets? Your competitors?

Preparing mentally for a dream is a double-dividend proposition. Not only are we getting ready to do a good job fulfilling our part of the dream when the door opens, but we're improving ourselves personally at the same time. We're better off, whether the door opens or not.

Dreams keep us young as we grow older. A friend who practices medicine told me chronological age sometimes has very little to do with how old a person is. His patients in their nineties are often "younger" than patients in their sixties because they still dream. The sad truth is that as many people grow older, they quit dreaming. This causes them to lack a sense of purpose, concentrate on their problems, focus on themselves, and act as though the shelf life on their brain has expired.

Write down resources available to you to help you learn more about the topic of your dream.

Preparing Physically for the Journey

Maybe you're wondering, *What in the world does preparing myself physically have to do with my dream, unless, of course, I'm dreaming of running in the Boston Marathon?* Actually, physical preparation has much more to do with turning a dream into reality than you might imagine.

God, of course, created our bodies, just as He created our minds and spirits. In fact, our bodies, minds, and souls are inextricably linked. We are whole people, not machines with interchangeable parts. If one part isn't working well, the others will surely feel the ill effects. And while many of our dreams probably won't involve winning the Boston

Marathon or single-handedly building a cathedral, being prepared physically means being at our own optimum condition (according to who we are, not compared to someone else's chart).

When we don't take care of our bodies—through exercise, eating wisely, taking vitamins, and drinking plenty of water—we have double trouble. First, our bodies get out of shape, which causes us to have less physical energy and be more susceptible to sickness. We're simply not in top condition to work toward our dream. We must be ready for the uphill climb ahead.

Second, when we have less energy, we also tend to feel bad about who we are and how we look, which drains us even more, especially of emotional energy. It's easy to get on a downward spiral: We don't eat properly; we don't exercise; we're too tired to take that class or read that book; and God will understand if we don't stay in touch with Him; besides, we're too ashamed to talk with Him since we've messed everything up. It's a trap we set for ourselves. Keeping in shape physically feeds emotional, mental, and spiritual fitness. But then keeping in shape spiritually does the same to us physically, mentally, emotionally, and so on.

If we're prepared spiritually and mentally, we'll feel more like making healthy, wise decisions every day about what we eat and drink and how we take care of our bodies. When the time comes to pursue our dream, we will be prepared.

And there's more good news. Being prepared physically has the same double-dividend benefit that

Growth Op

Start building up your energy bank account today. Begin small. If you're already in an exercise program, go that extra mile. If you've given up on taking care of yourself physically, begin with a twenty-minute, brisk walk every day. Consider getting an exercise book or consulting with a fitness expert at a YMCA or local gym.

being prepared mentally does. We're getting ready to do a good job fulfilling our part of the dream, but we're improving ourselves at the same time. Again, this is true whether the dream opens up or not.

Preparing Emotionally for the Journey

Taking care of our emotional health, like taking care of our physical health, is an ongoing, day-by-day process. No one's life is all sunshine. Sometimes we feel down in the dumps for an obvious reason, sometimes for no reason that we can determine. The point of taking care of our emotional health is not to feel happy all the time. Rather it's to recognize our feelings, to live with them. As a result we can live in a way that alleviates stress and allows us to deal better with whatever circumstances come our way.

No matter how big or small our dream is, we will be less efficient in pursuing it if we don't take care of ourselves. It'll take us longer to do simple tasks, and we'll often make mistakes, creating more work, which will take up even more time. We'll become emotionally stressed out when our dream does or doesn't come to pass.

Sometimes we think that pursuing a dream, or rather, having it come true, will solve all our emotional problems. Even if our dream is to solve emotional problems per se, like removing the discord in our family lives, we personally need to work toward getting into good emotional shape to pursue that dream. Remember two things: Pursuing God's dreams is hard, risky work; it's hardly ever status quo. And, if we're undertaking a dream simply to solve an emotional problem, it might be a good idea to take a second, third, and fourth prayerful look at that dream. Perhaps it's not a dream from God at all, but a dream born of our own neediness.

When we're not at our emotional best, it's sometimes hard to see the path in front of us well enough to take the first step. Most of us let ourselves go too long without rest, refreshment, and doing things that recharge our emotional batteries. All of a sudden we find ourselves close to the crash-and-burn stage, unable to manage our life, much less pursue our dream.

As we prepare ourselves to pursue a dream, emotional preparedness goes hand in hand with spiritual, mental, and physical preparedness.

Any Dream Needs Preparation

In our talk about dreams, we've concentrated quite a bit on implementing new ideas, making career changes, doing God's work. Sometimes a dream can be quite personal. Whatever the dream, we need to be prepared.

Recently, a young woman with a dream asked if we could talk. She explained that she was tired of being single. Every day, she dreamed of being married, of coming home at night to someone who loved her, of snuggling up to a warm body in bed. There's nothing wrong with these desires. It's just that as our conversation progressed, it seemed her dream of marriage revolved around what it would do for her, how being married would meet her needs. She also expected God to plop down her husband-to-be right in front of her, as she sat there and waited.

I asked her what she was doing to prepare herself to be a wife. Interestingly, she wasn't doing anything. We talked about how important it was for her to be growing spiritually so that she could be alert for God's leading and know when a certain man was the right one for her. We also discussed the importance of her being mentally, physically, and emotionally prepared for marriage.

She agreed there were many things she could do to prepare herself for the man of her dreams. Then I suggested one more thing: that she should "play in the traffic." She wouldn't get hit

Growth Op

What do you do in your spare time? How can you better prepare yourself for the journey of your dream? Have you
➠ been to a trade show or convention on the topic of your dream?
➠ bought any new books or tapes pertaining to your dream?
➠ gone out of your way to look for something that has to do with your dream?
➠ started a journal and recorded the steps you are taking toward your dream?
➠ told anyone else about your dream?
➠ prayed about your dream? How much?
➠ gone on a spiritual retreat?

sitting at home hoping Mr. Right would show up on her front doorstep. This line of thinking is tantamount to wishing a million dollars would show up in your bank account. She needed to get out and meet new people, get involved in community affairs and at church, work out at a gym, join professional associations.

> The problem of turning a dream into an opportunity is not a matter of manipulating God's hand, but rather of discovering the process God uses to transform us to prepare us for our destiny. He wants to prepare us so that we will honor Him with the opportunity He presents us to fulfill the dream that He's given us.

By the time we'd finished our second cup of coffee, she had a much clearer sense of her dream as a dream from God, a dream in which she could give of herself and be there for someone else (as well as having him be there for her). She also had a pageful of ideas to pursue to prepare herself. And, I hope, as she pursued her spiritual preparation, a sense of who she is and could become in God's eyes, whether the door to her marriage dream opens or not.

CHAPTER 11

The Prayer Component

Pray to God, but row toward the shore.

RUSSIAN PROVERB

The reason you don't have what you want is that you don't ask God for it.

JAMES 4:2, TLB

Prayer is the key that unlocks the storehouse of God's riches. Dreaming requires imagination. Taking a dream from idea to opportunity requires wisdom—often, a lot of wisdom. In Nehemiah's mind, wisdom dictated two responsibilities: prayer and planning. It's no different for us. Whatever situation we find ourselves in, no matter how farfetched our dreams may seem, nothing and no one can prevent us from praying and planning for our dreams to come true. Because prayer is so essential at every inch along the road from dream to reality, we'll spend a lot of time on the subject.

As hard as we may work, and as much influence as we may acquire, nothing happens without prayer. It is the call that moves heaven to act on behalf of earth. If I have a dream, and I want to see that dream come true, I must learn to pray. Christ made this clear in John 15:5: "Apart from me you can do nothing." Prayer is the first step wisdom demands of us when we dream.

> More things are wrought by prayer than this world dreams of.
>
> —ALFRED LORD TENNYSON

Before we delve into this critical component of turning a dream into an opportunity, let's make sure we're on the same page—literally and figuratively. We're talking about praying during the process of turning dreams into opportunities, about dependence on God and responsible action, about praying and working while we're praying. As Saint Benedict's motto "Work is prayer" so wisely puts it, planning for our dreams and working on them is a kind of prayer.

> You can commit no greater folly than to sit by the roadside until someone comes along and invites you to ride with him to wealth or influence.
>
> —JOHN B. GOUGH

A Critical Dreaming Ingredient

The apostle Paul, the greatest evangelist the world has ever known, had a really big dream. He dreamed not only of evangelizing the world, but also about the spiritual transformation of the people he evangelized. He described his dream like this: "We proclaim him, admonishing and teaching everyone with all wisdom, so that we may present everyone perfect in Christ. To this end I labor, struggling with all his energy, which so powerfully works within me" (Colossians 1:28-29).

Paul was a strong and charismatic person. If ever there was an individual who could have forced his dreams into reality by sheer intensity of will, or compelled men and women to change by pure impact of personal dynamism, or convinced people by raw strength of mental competence, it was Paul. But we find Paul consistently praying while he was working toward his God-given dreams.

> *For this reason, since the day we heard about you, we have not stopped praying for you and asking God to fill you with the knowledge of his will through all spiritual wisdom and understanding. And we pray this in order that you may live a life worthy of the Lord and may please him in every way: bearing fruit in every good work, growing in the knowledge of God, being strengthened with all power according to his glorious might so that you may have great endurance and patience, and joyfully giving thanks to the Father, who has qualified you to share in the inheritance of the saints in the kingdom of light. (Colossians 1:9-12)*

Paul recognized that he could never effect the change he desired apart from God's hand working in the lives of people. He knew that not one person would take one step toward maturity apart from the intervening will of God. So it's not surprising that he was not bashful in asking others to pray for him.

Devote yourselves to prayer, being watchful and thank-ful. And pray for us, too, that God may open a door for our message, so that we may proclaim the mystery of Christ, for which I am in chains. Pray that I may pro-claim it clearly, as I should. (Colossians 4:2-4)

William Wilberforce, member of the English parliament in the nineteenth century, is another man who understood the importance of prayer. He dreamed of a day when the sun would rise on an empire of free men and women. In his quixotic, fifty-year quest to end slavery in the British Empire, Wilberforce knew that all of his political influence, personal wealth, and persuasive talent could not make his dream come true. So, together with a small group of his peers, he prayed.

Valdemar Hvidt, a Danish attorney, dreamed of eliminating unemployment at the height of the great depression in Denmark.

Have I committed myself to con-sistently pray for my dream?

With little prospect of success, Hvidt convened a group of associates and began praying for guidance about how to solve this impossible prob-lem. As a result, they implemented new ideas that resulted in thousands of new jobs. When Nazi occupation ended their efforts in 1939, Hvidt's group became the core of the Danish resistance.

Benjamin Franklin dreamed of a nation of united states. When the Constitutional Convention reached an impasse, Franklin called the delegates to convene with daily prayer and commit their work to the Lord. He wisely cautioned them,

I have lived a long time, and the longer I live the more convincing proof I see of this truth, that God governs in the affairs of men. If a sparrow cannot fall to the ground without His notice, is it probable that an empire can rise without His aid? We have been assured in the Sacred Writings that "Except the Lord build the house, they labor in vain that build it." I firmly believe that

without His concurring aid we shall proceed in this
political building no better than the builders of Babel.[1]

Praying Our Dreams

Nehemiah understood the importance of prayer. Left initially with no other prospects of changing the situation in Jerusalem, he prayed. There's a great deal of wisdom we can learn from him about praying our dreams.

Focus on the One Who Hears Our Prayers

There's no doubt that our knowledge of God and understanding of what He desires us to do temper our prayers. We often miss God's best because we fail to ask according to the greatness of His character and might.

It's no coincidence that most of the prayers in the Bible, including Nehemiah's, begin with worship, recognizing and acknowledging the character of God. You see, the size of our God will determine the size of our dreams and requests. If we know and understand that God is truly "able to do exceeding abundantly beyond all we ask or think," then we will tend to dream great dreams about what God might do in this world, because we know that heaven is not limited by earthly obstacles and dilemmas or any limitations we might have personally. Because Nehemiah knew God to be a great, awesome, promise-keeping God, he dared to dream that the walls could be rebuilt.

• •

We tread altogether too gingerly on the great and precious promises of God and too often we ignore them wholly. The promise is the ground on which faith stands in asking of God. This is the one basis of prayer. We limit God's ability. We measure God's ability and willingness to answer prayer by the standards of men.

—E. M. BOUNDS, AMERICAN THEOLOGIAN

Growth Op

Take a moment right now to consider some things that God has revealed about Himself in His Word.

He is eager to answer, without reluctance.
> Before they call I will answer;
> while they are still speaking I will hear. (Isaiah 65:24)

He is incredibly generous, giving more than we ask or deserve.
> Blessed be the Lord,
> who daily loads us with benefits,
> the God of our salvation! (Psalm 68:19, authors' paraphrase)

He is absolutely good.
> Which of you, if his son asks for bread, will give him a stone? . . . If you, then, though you are evil, know how to give good gifts to your children, how much more will your Father in heaven give good gifts to those who ask him! (Matthew 7:9,11)

He is in complete control.
> All the peoples of the earth
> are regarded as nothing.
> He does as he pleases
> with the powers of heaven
> and the peoples of the earth.
> No one can hold back his hand
> or say to him: "What have you done?" (Daniel 4:35)

Prayer is not conquering God's reluctance, but taking hold of God's willingness.

—Phillip Brooks, American theologian (1835–1893)

Don't Sidestep God's Holiness

One of the hazards of seeking God is actually meeting up with Him. Those who have gotten a glimpse of Him are struck with two conflicting desires—one to draw closer to the utter beauty they see, and the other to run in horror because of the ugliness of sin it reveals in themselves. That attribute of absolute perfection in God is His holiness. It is what simultaneously attracts us to and repels us from God.

Sinful men and women cannot approach a holy God apart from His grace and our willingness to confess our sinful failures. Because of this, Nehemiah wastes no time in moving from adoration to confession.

> *I confess the sins we Israelites, including myself and my father's house, have committed against you. We have acted very wickedly toward you. We have not obeyed the commands, decrees and laws you gave your servant Moses. (Nehemiah 1:6-7)*

Nehemiah's confession reminds us of three things. First, repentance is the work of good men and women. It's not surprising to find these verses in Nehemiah's prayer since repentance was a condition God required before He would restore the Jews to the Promised Land. Even though numerous Jews had been able to return to a Jerusalem in ruins, Nehemiah knew the process wasn't complete. What is surprising is that Nehemiah includes himself in the confession. Without a doubt, one of the hardest phrases to utter in any human language is, "I am wrong." But godly men and women have no trouble admitting their faults. No matter how good we might be, we all still fall short of what God expects of us. In fact, men and women who are truly close to God are more aware of their sins than any wicked people. That makes pride and arrogance impossible for those who are really walking with God.

Second, God doesn't owe us anything but justice. Because we fall short of God's standards, the only thing we can demand of God is judgment. When we come to a holy God with our dreams, we ask in spite of our behavior, not because we deserve it. We can only come to God on the basis of His mercy and grace. Because His mercy and grace are true, we echo the writer of the letter to the Hebrews: "Let us then approach the throne of grace with confidence, so that we may receive mercy and find grace to help us in our time of need" (Hebrews 4:16).

Third, we need to acknowledge our sin and accept Christ's forgiveness. If we don't, we may stand personally in the way of our dream. God has not pledged Himself to keep disobedient people happy and fulfilled in their dreams. To do so would be a tragedy beyond imagining. The most unkind thing that God could do for men and women on a course of sin would be to ensure their happiness and contentment, leaving their path uninterrupted. The most unkind thing we can do to ourselves is wallow in guilt that God has forgiven. The pride that refuses God's forgiveness will ruin us and our dream, and throttle our relationship with God.

Base Your Prayer on the Promises of God's Word

Dreaming is not about trying to get a celestial genie to grant our wishes, nor is effective prayer manipulating God to give us what we want. It is asking a generous God to accomplish His purposes through us. It's requesting that He make us part of what He already plans to do. The more we understand His Word, the better we will know His will — and pray according to it. Christ promised, "If you remain in me and my words remain in you, ask whatever you wish, and it will be given you" (John 15:7).

When Nehemiah prayed, he didn't wish, speculate, or guess what God's will was for Jerusalem. He knew. As busy as Nehemiah was, he found time to discover God's specific promises for Jewish restoration revealed in the Bible.

Let's face it. There is never enough time to do everything we want to do, including studying the Word of God. But searching God's Word is not so much a matter of priority as it is a matter of survival. In my own life, when I recognize my desperate need of guidance and wisdom and understand God's eagerness to give, I have no trouble digging into the Bible. Nehemiah must have felt like Abraham Lincoln during the dark days of the Civil War. Lincoln wrote, "I have been driven many times upon my knees by the overwhelming conviction that I had nowhere else to go." Confronted with the dark days in Jerusalem, Nehemiah went to God's Word for answers and found God's promise recorded in Deuteronomy 28–30. So he asked accordingly,

> *Remember the instruction you gave your servant Moses, saying, "If you are unfaithful, I will scatter you among the nations, but if you return to me and obey my commands, then even if your exiled people are at the farthest horizon, I will gather them from there and bring them to the place I have chosen as a dwelling for my Name." (Nehemiah 1:8-9)*

Never Stop Praying

When answers don't come and our dreams sit in neutral, there is a tremendous tendency to doubt God's goodness. From our limited perspective, it seems so crystal clear what should be done. But we should always remember to hold our perspective with some degree of skepticism. Only God sees the whole picture. Only He has the wisdom to know exactly the best way and the best timing to accomplish His good purpose for us.

Search the Scripture for insights that tell you specifically how to pray for your dream. Use the *NIV Topical Study Bible*. Look for subjects that have to do with your dream, such as courage, strength, perseverance, integrity, patience, and money.

I am convinced that there is always a good reason for a delay. Perhaps what we dream about is not the best thing. Though God loves to answer the prayers of His children, there are times when we ask for things that would not be good for us or the world. And we can never cajole or weary God into giving us less than what is best. I may give in to my boys' nagging, but God is never tired by our whining. Sometimes the timing is just not right. When the answer to a prayer is delayed, most of the time I've found that God has something He wants to do in my heart.

Sam Shoemaker, cofounder of Alcoholics Anonymous, once said, "Prayer may not change things for you, but it for sure changes you for things." Continuing in prayer does change us. Many times God is working to enlarge our faith and intensify our commitment to the dream, preparing us for the sacrifice ahead that we will have to make. Much of the time in my life it seems that God is wrestling the ownership of His dream from my hands, making sure that I am more committed to Him than the dream He has given. Whatever the reason, the Bible tells us not to give up, but to keep praying. "Then Jesus told his disciples a parable to show them that they should always pray and not give up" (Luke 18:1).

Instead of causing us to give up, delay should intensify our asking. If asking does not get it, we should send out a search party, earnestly seeking the Lord. If seeking does not do it, we need to move to noisy knocking, earnestly persevering until we have what we want.

Watch Where You Put Your Hope

If you're like me, you have a tendency to latch hold of the answer you desire rather than the One who answers. This is dangerous. I've learned it's all too easy for my hope to move subtly from God to the fulfillment of my dream. When this happens, God may delay His answer to my prayer so that my hope will return to Him. He may also see that what I request is not best, or that there is a better way to accomplish what I really desire.

If we become fixated on the dream rather than God, I guarantee our faith will be shaken. We need to be on guard constantly and remember with David that God is our only hope.

No one whose hope is in you
will ever be put to shame,
but they will be put to shame
who are treacherous without excuse.

Show me your ways, O LORD,
teach me your paths;
guide me in your truth and teach me,

for you are God my Savior,
and my hope is in you all day long. (Psalm 25:3-5)

Make God's Glory Your Ultimate Goal

When we follow great men and women of prayer through the Bible and history, we find that they concern themselves with God's glory. They want others to recognize God's greatness and power. That's a servant's concern, isn't it—not the glory of the servant but the exaltation of his master? If you haven't noticed, the words *servant* or *servants* are used eight times in Nehemiah's prayer. There's no confusion in Nehemiah's mind about who's in charge and who gets the glory. Here is a portion of that prayer:

> *Hear the prayer your* servant *is praying before you day and night for your* servants, *the people of Israel. . . . They are your* servants *and your people, whom you redeemed by your great strength and your mighty hand. O Lord, let your ear be attentive to the prayer of this your* servant *and to the prayer of your* servants *who delight in revering your name. Give your* servant *success today by granting him favor in the presence of this man. (Nehemiah 1:6,10-11,* emphasis added*)*

Perhaps the reason so many of our prayers are ineffective is that we have our roles reversed. I must admit, I have prayed many prayers where I was more concerned with what people thought of me than with God's reputation and glory. It's not that my actual requests were necessarily bad or even selfish. It's just that I was more interested in people knowing who I am than who God is.

> Men may spurn our appeals, reject our message, oppose our arguments, despise our persons, but they are helpless against our prayers.
>
> —J. SIDLOW BAXTOR,
> AMERICAN THEOLOGIAN

The consuming passion behind every prayer request we make should be God's glory. James reminds us how important this is:

147

> The one concern of the devil is to keep saints from prayer. He fears nothing from prayerless studies, prayerless work, prayerless religion. He laughs at our toil, mocks at our wisdom, but trembles when we pray.
>
> —SAMUEL CHADWICK, QUOTED BY E. M. BOUNDS, *THE POSSIBILITIES OF PRAYER*

"When you ask, you do not receive, because you ask with wrong motives, that you may spend what you get on your pleasures" (James 4:3).

Don't miss the point—God has nothing against pleasure. He invented it. But pleasure is a gift from God, not a goal. It's God's pleasure that should be the focus of our prayer. If my own interests or status is what really drives me, I'm inviting the delay of my dream. And it's a sure bet, if it comes, it will never be enough to satisfy me.

God made us by nature servants, and we can never know fulfillment seeking our own glory. We were made for God's pleasure and His glory. God's glory is not only the motive behind effective prayer, it is always in our best interest as well.

The Most Important Element

Growth Op

Read Matthew 18:19-20. Is there anyone who can join you in praying for your dream?

Whatever else we might leave out of this process of dreaming, we can't leave out the focus of this chapter—prayer. There's no more potent force in transforming passions to dreams, dreams to opportunities, and opportunities to realities.

CHAPTER

Planning for Progress

Suppose one of you wants to build a tower. Will he not first sit down and estimate the cost to see if he has enough money to complete it?

JESUS CHRIST, LUKE 14:28

Men don't plan to fail— they fail to plan.

WILLIAM J. SIEGEL, CORPORATE EXECUTIVE (1910–1966)

Bill was born in Texas, raised in Texas, and I thought he'd live there all his life. When somebody asks his nationality, he responds, "Texan." He has been known to send out "Happy Texas Independence Day" cards on March 2. If you had asked me five years ago if Bill would ever willingly move from Texas, I would have laughed. You can live with a person for over twenty-five years; eat thousands of meals together; bring three boys into the world together; attend about a million soccer, baseball, football, and basketball games together; and get to the point where you finish each other's sentences; but you can still be surprised by what goes on in this other person's brain.

When Bill told me he was dreaming of moving to Nashville, Tennessee, I sat there stunned and speechless. (And I am a person who almost always has something to say.) I was stunned for two reasons: First, never in a million years did I think Bill would want to leave Texas. The second reason was almost eerie, because for some time I had harbored the same dream. God, as the old saying goes, does work in mysterious ways.

As we talked that morning, we shared that we were both growing weary of the two-and-a-half-hour commute to the Dallas airport. Increasingly, my work was taking me out of town to speak. We concurred that every time we visited Nashville to see my agent or call on friends, we fell more in love with the beauty of the city and the area. We realized it would be much more convenient for me and my work if we lived there. Plus, we would be much closer to my parents, who live in Memphis—a benefit for all of us.

It would be an understatement to say there were a few obstacles. And at first, the barriers are what we thought of. We couldn't afford to just pick up and move. We'd have to uproot our kids from school. We'd have to sell our house in Texas where the market was down and buy one in Nashville where the market was hot. Bill had founded a ministry in Texas and would have to give that up and find another job. The obstacles seemed—and were to the objective observer— huge. But our mutual dream was strong within us. So we prayed.

150

And as we prayed, we remembered that things that seem impossible in human eyes aren't in God's. We prayed, and our dream remained strong. We began to see that God may well have ideas we'd never imagined.

We started to plan. We made a list of subjects we needed to research: real estate, schools, the cost of living. We got information from Nashville. We started putting out feelers for possible job opportunities for Bill. We worked for weeks to gather all the information we could. We wanted to be ready when God opened the door. Finally, we took a deep breath and put our house in Tyler on the market.

It's amazing that we who call ourselves people of faith, children of a living God who cares intimately about every detail of our lives, are so surprised when He answers our prayers. Within weeks Bill learned of a job opportunity that would allow him to live in Nashville — and even pay for us to move there. (It was a concrete reminder that God often gives us more than we ask for.) We started to look for houses and schools for the children in Nashville. But even though things were beginning to fall into place, the key to our dream coming true was selling the house in Tyler. It wasn't selling. Yet we continued to pray and plan and, at the end of four months, it sold. We bought a house in Nashville and moved.

It all started with a dream, but that dream couldn't have come to pass if we hadn't prayed and planned.

If you have a dream you believe to be from God, the question is not *if*, but *when* and *how* God will open the door and turn that dream into a real opportunity. To be fully ready, we would do well to follow Nehemiah's example and have a tentative plan in mind, even before we need it.

Nehemiah Had a Plan in Hand

From the outset Nehemiah prayed, but as soon as his dream began to take shape, he began doing his homework. When the Lord opened the door, Nehemiah was ready with a well-thought-through plan. Over time, Nehemiah's dream had developed into a detailed vision with clear steps and schedules. When the king asked, Nehemiah was ready with details.

> *Then the king . . . asked me, "How long will your journey take, and when will you get back?" It pleased the king to send me; so I set a time.*
>
> *I also said to him, "If it pleases the king, may I have letters to the governors of Trans-Euphrates, so that they will provide me safe-conduct until I arrive in Judah? And may I have a letter to Asaph, keeper of the king's forest, so he will give me timber to make beams for the gates of the citadel by the temple and for the city wall and for the residence I will occupy?" And because the gracious hand of my God was upon me, the king granted my requests. (Nehemiah 2:6-8)*

Planning is far from presumptuous. Planning what needs to happen for our dream to become reality is an act of faith. If you believe that God has given you a dream, it's time to plan—right now. Do you see any opportunities opening up on the horizon? Even if you don't, if it's God's dream, you should begin to plan for it to happen.

As we look back on our lives, we see that we've missed the chance to walk through open doors of opportunity because we were unprepared or afraid. We really didn't believe God would open them.

We haven't met anyone yet who likes to waste his or her efforts, to use time, money, and energy to no avail. But being prepared is one of the prime biblical directives given to us as Christians. We can't afford not to be ready. Whereas people or circumstances can keep us from moving forward in our dreams, nothing stands between us and prayer and planning—nothing, that is, except our lack of faith and self-discipline.

Nehemiah knew he would appeal to the king when the time arrived, and he had a list ready. These are important elements of any plan, and it would behoove us to follow Nehemiah's example.

Nehemiah planned his appeal to the king. Although not explicitly stated, Nehemiah responded with such precision and detail it seems clear his threefold response had been prepared: "But I said to the king, 'May the king live forever! Why should my face not look sad when the city where my fathers are buried lies in ruins, and its gates have been destroyed by fire?'" (2:3).

Notice how Nehemiah appealed to the king. First, he assured the king of his loyalty. There was no plot to kill or undermine the king. Nehemiah wished nothing but long life and God's favor on him. Nehemiah was committed to serving and pleasing his master, not running off on some idealistic crusade in disregard of the king's will.

Second, Nehemiah wisely made his request in the terms the king would most likely understand and identify with, thus demonstrating that he empathized with the king's desires, feelings, and priorities. He certainly could have taken a different tack. Remember, this was the ruler most recently responsible for the dismal situation in Jerusalem that so grieved Nehemiah. Nehemiah chose his words carefully. He could have attacked the king—"You're the reason I'm sad. It's your fault. Don't you know Jerusalem is God's city?"—and he would have been right. Dead right. He could have appealed to the king politically—"Wouldn't it be advantageous to have a loyal man between your two enemies Syria and Egypt? Let me establish a loyal outpost for you in Jerusalem." Instead, he left this conclusion to the king's own political acumen. He appealed to the king's personal sentiments and religious convictions. Everywhere in the East, ancestors and their graves are revered—even today. This is how Nehemiah wisely chose to couch his request.

Third, notice that Nehemiah appealed to the quality of their relationship and his work as a basis for his request.

> *The king said to me, "What is it you want?"*
> *Then I prayed to the God of heaven, and I answered the king, "If it pleases the king and if your servant has found favor in his sight, let him send me to the city in Judah where my fathers are buried so that I can rebuild it."*
> *(2:4-5)*

When thinking about the future and longing for it, we've got to keep our feet firmly planted in the reality of the present. The reason Nehemiah wasn't shipped off immediately to the lions' den, the reason the king stopped to listen and opened the door for Nehemiah to explain his dream, lay not only in the sovereign hand of God but also in Nehemiah's faithful and excellent work over years of service. The fact is, many times the quality of our work will either open or close doors for us, as the proverbist implies:

• •

Do you see a man skilled in his work?
He will serve before kings;
    he will not serve before obscure men.

—PROVERBS 22:29

Nehemiah also had a number of details already worked out in his mind. First, he knew his role in the project—he was going to be in charge, the person of responsibility. It was *his* project and the buck stopped with him. Why was that important? Because every dream needs a champion. Every opportunity needs a leader, someone to make it happen.

Second, Nehemiah knew what he needed to make the project a success. The three things he required are identical to what every person needs for success.

➠ *Authority:* He had to ask to be sent. He had to have the authority to do what he wanted to do.

➠ *Security:* He asked for a letter from the king guaranteeing him safe passage.

➠ *Resources:* He asked for the authority to requisition materials.

And third, Nehemiah had a time schedule. He knew his time frame. When he was asked how long it would take, he was ready with an answer.

Nehemiah was a man of wisdom. He knew that in God's sovereign will, it took human and divine resources working together to bring a dream to reality, and he skillfully combined his human resources with the divine resources given to him to bring his dream to the point of opportunity.

He recognized that his success was from God. Wise men and women know that as much and as hard as they work, they can't ensure that what they want to happen will actually take place. Nehemiah knew that God worked all things after the counsel of His will, that the reason he was given this opportunity was because God opened the door for him. He is very clear about this: "Because the gracious hand of my God was upon me, the king granted my requests" (Nehemiah 2:8).

As we look back from a historical perspective at what God did, it was no coincidence that there was a Jew in a court of the king—a Jew who dreamed that God would fulfill His promises and purposes outlined long ago to Moses about the restoration of God's people. It was also no coincidence that the political situation at this time made it advantageous for the king to have a loyal man stationed in the land that separated Egypt and Syria—rising rivals to the west. God moved in Nehemiah's

Ask yourself the following questions to begin assembling the elements of your plan for your dream.

➭ Who? Who needs to be involved? Whose authority do I need? Who will be affected by my dream?

➭ What? What specifically do I want to happen? What needs to be done?

➭ Where? What is the setting? What are the options?

➭ When? When will it happen? Are there deadlines?

➭ Why? What is the purpose behind the dream? What are the most important reasons this should happen?

➭ How? What are the steps I see at this point?

➭ How much? How much time will it take? How much money? How many resources? How much will it demand of my relationships?

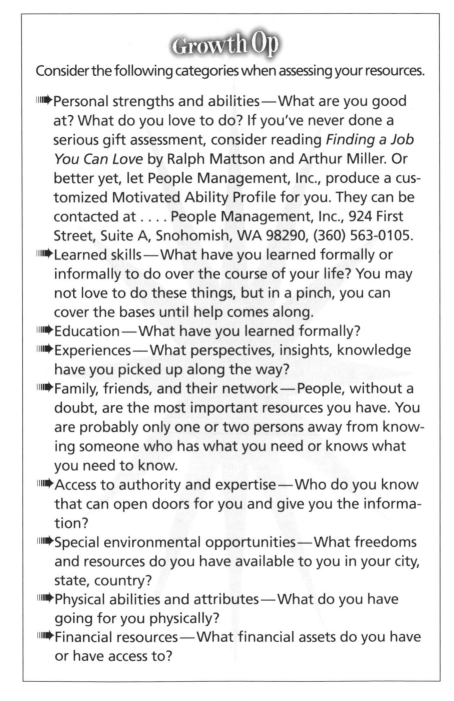

Growth Op

Consider the following categories when assessing your resources.

➡ Personal strengths and abilities—What are you good at? What do you love to do? If you've never done a serious gift assessment, consider reading *Finding a Job You Can Love* by Ralph Mattson and Arthur Miller. Or better yet, let People Management, Inc., produce a customized Motivated Ability Profile for you. They can be contacted at . . . . People Management, Inc., 924 First Street, Suite A, Snohomish, WA 98290, (360) 563-0105.

➡ Learned skills—What have you learned formally or informally to do over the course of your life? You may not love to do these things, but in a pinch, you can cover the bases until help comes along.

➡ Education—What have you learned formally?

➡ Experiences—What perspectives, insights, knowledge have you picked up along the way?

➡ Family, friends, and their network—People, without a doubt, are the most important resources you have. You are probably only one or two persons away from knowing someone who has what you need or knows what you need to know.

➡ Access to authority and expertise—Who do you know that can open doors for you and give you the information?

➡ Special environmental opportunities—What freedoms and resources do you have available to you in your city, state, country?

➡ Physical abilities and attributes—What do you have going for you physically?

➡ Financial resources—What financial assets do you have or have access to?

heart, and He also carefully orchestrated the political situation in the world so that the king would be predisposed to Nehemiah's request. Nehemiah prepared himself; he prayed; he waited; he planned. He was able to turn his dream into a real opportunity.

Recognizing Resources

One of the most important aspects of planning for your dream is being able to assess and gather the appropriate resources needed to make your dream a reality. Each of us has an impressive array of personal, divinely endowed strengths as well as external resources that God has placed at our disposal. As you plan, spend much more time focusing on your strengths and resources than on your weaknesses and shortcomings. Focusing on weakness will give you a tenuous grip on the reality of the true situation, clouding your vision, causing you to miss much of what God has for you.

Key to recognizing your resources is making sure your dream is clear in your mind. The sharpness of your dream will determine to a large degree the visibility of resources you have all around you. Dreaming makes you aware of resources you never knew you had.

Don't concentrate on what you don't have. If you don't have it, quite frankly, you don't need it —yet. If this is God's dream, you can count on Him to provide all that you need to accomplish His will in His timing.

And pray, pray, pray. Don't forget to ask God to provide what you need. Remember what the apostle Paul told the Philippians: "And my God will meet all your needs according to his glorious riches in Christ Jesus" (Philippians 4:19).

Reckoning with Roadblocks

It's an imperfect, fallen world. There are barriers ahead of us that we must face before we can turn our dreams into realities. If we want to see our dreams come to pass, we can't stay in dreamland.

We must be totally realistic about what we and those we take with us on the road to our dream will face ahead. We will certainly not be able to see every pothole in the road or know what's coming around every bend, but we can eliminate as many obstacles as possible that we see right now by planning effectively.

From where Nehemiah stood, he saw three major obstacles: a scarcity of building materials immediately available to complete the job; a potential challenge to his authority, as well as a safety risk from Jerusalem's neighbors; and an uncertain labor pool. By sizing these roadblocks up realistically ahead of time, Nehemiah was able to make plans to neutralize their effect.

Types of Roadblocks to Consider

Consider the following categories as you assess the obstacles that stand in the way of your dream. Be sure to label each one actual, probable, or potential, and remember, don't be pessimistic.

Personal limitations—Everyone has them. Yes, it's true. God didn't create any of us to do it all. That means that there will be glaring gaps in our competency that we will need others to bridge. Don't fret trying to make yourself good at something God just didn't put in your bag of tricks. That's the worst possible waste of time and energy. Do what you are good at and trust God to find others to do what they are good at to fill in the gaps. To do otherwise is to question the Creator's design.

Lack of certain skills—Again, this is to be expected. Are the skills crucial to the success of the venture? Can you train yourself or be trained to do them? Can you limp along doing things poorly until you can do things right?

Schedule and time problems—There are only twenty-four hours in every day. Time is a built-in human constraint that we must accept. The fact is that we will never have enough time to ensure success or safety. Remember what David says,

Unless the LORD builds the house,
They labor in vain who build it;

Unless the LORD guards the city,
The watchman keeps awake in vain.
It is vain for you to rise up early,
To retire late,
To eat the bread of painful labors;
For He gives to His beloved even in his sleep.
  (Psalm 127:1-2, NASB)

It is possible, however, to be so busy with the details of life that we don't have time to do the most important things. Some ruthless assessment of our schedules is in order for most of us.

Habits—Addictions, fixations, hang-ups plague us all. It's possible for one or more to be a major obstacle you must overcome. Unlike personal limitations, which are God-imposed, these are self-imposed. Procrastination, anger, self-indulgence, and a host of other tendencies can stand in the way of our dreams. They can be faced and conquered by God's power and with the help of a supportive group of peers.

Physical limitations—There are certain things I just can't do physically. I can dream all day about having a baby, but it just won't happen. God didn't physically equip men to bear children—thank goodness! I have to accept that personally, but I can still dream about having children since God brought Kathy and me together.

Finances—Every so often I hear of someone who is not faced with financial barriers. I'm not sure, but I think that person is a myth. Most people I know have to deal creatively (legally, of course) with finances to get their dream moving forward.

People—Sad to say, but the very ones God put here to help us fulfill our dreams are often the ones who dash them to the floor. Wives, husbands, mothers, fathers, siblings, associates, competitors, enemies—all can raise significant barriers. Some should be resisted, others accepted and prayed for.

Keys to Dealing with Roadblocks

When assessing the roadblocks to your plan, don't blow them out of proportion. When we start counting problems, they have a way of making unbelievers of us all. Just the other day I took a look at my schedule and time commitments during the time we have left to finish this book. I started thinking about all the work still uncompleted and I have to confess I was totally overwhelmed and immobilized. I had let the enlarging machine of my mind blow things totally out of proportion. I stepped back and decided to take things one step at a time and am making good progress. Kathy and I also began to pray daily together as we've never prayed before for wisdom and guidance. It's amazing how small roadblocks get when compared to the size of our God.

> If you go out looking for trouble, you'll find it.

Don't invent roadblocks. One of the worst things I do is worry about what might be. I'm convinced that we waste a lot of energy worrying about potential problems that never materialize. It's good to expect possible roadblocks before you meet them, but don't spend time agonizing over what to do about them. Nehemiah had two real and one possible problem. He spent time on the two, materials and safety, but he made no provision for the third, a labor-force problem. It was certainly possible that the Jews in Jerusalem would not cooperate, but Nehemiah chose not to invest in a problem before it actually materialized.

Budget spartanly for problems. Spend a very limited amount of time, energy, and resources on attempting to remove an obstacle. The lion's share of your energy and resources can more effectively be spent on enhancing strengths.

> A good plan today is better than a perfect plan tomorrow.
>
> —General George Patton

Final Words

Whatever barriers you face as you plan to pursue your dream, however, don't wait for all the answers or for all your ducks to get lined up. If you do, your dreams will go with you to the grave.

CHAPTER 13

The Waiting Game

*All things come to him who waits —
provided that he knows what he's
waiting for. If we sit around and wait
for something to turn up, it may not be
anything but our toes.*

WOODROW WILSON

*Patience and tenacity of purpose
are worth more than twice their weight
of cleverness.*

THOMAS HENRY HUXLEY, ENGLISH BIOLOGIST (1825–1895)

As a boy I never played golf, but living with a son who dreams of wearing a green jacket as winner of the Masters golf tournament someday, I've learned a lot about the culture of the game. As one saying goes, "If larceny is in the heart, golf will bring it out." It seems the desire to win is so strong and the opportunity to cheat, even if just a little, so great that shaving a few points off your score is hard to resist. I guess that's why I was so impressed when I read about Tom Lehman calling a penalty shot on himself in the 1990 qualifying school (Q-school, as the pros call it) for the PGA Tour. It seems a stiff breeze caused Lehman's ball to move slightly after he addressed it. The rules are clear. If the ball moves, you are penalized one stroke. If the most important thing in Lehman's life was his dream of qualifying for the tour, he might have responded differently. But his faith in Christ and his commitment to integrity called him to honesty. Unfortunately, Lehman missed the cut for the tour by one stroke. He would have to wait another year for a chance to qualify.

If Lehman had fudged, he would have had his dream, the fame, and a chance at millions of dollars, but at a tremendous price to him personally and to his ultimate dream. Lehman explained it like this: "If a breach of the rules had occurred and I didn't call it on myself, I couldn't look at myself in the mirror. You're only as good as your word. And your word wouldn't be worth much if you can't even be honest with yourself."[1]

> Prefer a loss to a dishonest gain; the one brings pain at the moment, the other for all time.
>
> —CHILTON

Lehman's loss at the Q-school sent him in 1991 to what's now known as the Nike Tour, where he set a tour record with seven tournament wins in a single season. The confidence he gained while waiting for his dream led to his two PGA Tour victories and status as one of the world's best golfers. I think Tom Lehman would say it was worth the wait.

The Importance of Perseverance

When we dream, not only do we need to keep our feet firmly planted in the present, but we also need to avoid being so consumed by our dream that we're willing to compromise God's standards to make it happen. When our dreams face continual delays, there is a tremendous temptation to move ahead of God and compulsively use our gifts to accomplish *His* dreams on *our* time schedule. When we do, we are sure to miss God's blessing—even though it's His dream. When things aren't happening according to our schedule, we need to persevere patiently until God opens the door.

• •

Living is like working out a long addition sum, and if you make a mistake in the first two totals, you will never find out the right answer.

—Cesare Pavese, Italian poet

One of the most tragic examples of impetuousness in the Bible is Moses' first attempt to deliver Israel. Even though he had the right dream, he impulsively moved ahead of God's timing. When we do that, we not only violate God's will in timing but usually compromise God's standards as well. When Moses tried to implement the dream in his own way in his own time, the results were disastrous.

One day, after Moses had grown up, he went out to where his own people were and watched them at their hard labor. He saw an Egyptian beating a Hebrew, one of his own people. Glancing this way and that and seeing no one, he killed the Egyptian and hid him in the sand. The next day he went out and saw two Hebrews fighting. He asked the one in the wrong, "Why are you hitting your fellow Hebrew?"

The man said, "Who made you ruler and judge over us? Are you thinking of killing me as you killed the

Egyptian?" Then Moses was afraid and thought, "What I did must have become known."

When Pharaoh heard of this, he tried to kill Moses, but Moses fled from Pharaoh and went to live in Midian, where he sat down by a well. (Exodus 2:11-15)

It took God forty years to retool and restore this man before He could use him again. And then it took a burning bush to get Moses to return to do God's work in God's time.

• •

There is no such thing as preaching patience into people unless the sermon is so long they have to practice it while they hear. No man can learn patience except by going out into the hurly-burly world, and taking life just as it blows. Patience is but lying to and riding out the gale.

—HENRY WARD BEECHER, AMERICAN CLERGYMAN (1813–1887)

I talked with a young man recently who has a strong sense of mission from God and vision for a certain ministry to which he has committed himself. Unfortunately, he is consumed by the vision rather than God. How can I make that judgment? Because, to him, keeping his vision foremost and progressing is more important than his ethical behavior. His "cause" justifies certain compromises of integrity. We should note it was Italian political philosopher Niccolò Machiavelli, not Jesus, who taught that the ends justify the means.

If you find yourself trying to make a dream happen yourself, you'll be tempted to shave a point here or there. If you do, you can be sure that your dream has become your god, in place of God Himself.

Nehemiah probably faced similar temptations to run ahead of God, get things moving, and make it happen. But he didn't. He waited and prayed, prepared himself for almost four months, and left the job of opening the door to God. God's

• •

I am extraordinarily patient provided I get my own way in the end.

—MARGARET THATCHER

timing is critical and must be honored if we want to honor Him in our dream. I don't care how big a success we become, God will not be honored if we run ahead of Him.

As far as God is concerned, perseverance, or patience in waiting, is an important ingredient in shaping the dreamer. It settles three issues.

Perseverance Settles the Ownership Issue

When we dream even godly dreams, the great temptation is to own those dreams for ourselves. Waiting forces our hand. When our dream is first crystallized, passions run deep. Internally we hunger for the fulfillment of our dreams, and yet there is unbearable delay in the "kitchen." As we wait and begin to despair of our dreams ever coming into existence, we have an opportunity to take a step of faith and put that dream into God's hands—where, of course, it is the safest anyway.

Although I shake my head at Mrs. Thatcher's attitude, I should probably confess to feeling the same way more times than I'm comfortable with the world knowing. I don't know how many times God has had to take me to the point of desperation where I'll finally say, "Lord, if You want this to take place, then You bring it about. It's Yours. I give up." When it finally dawns on me that I can't make happen the things I've been clutching, I open my hands and release them to God. I follow the advice of Proverbs 3:6: "In everything you do, put God first, and he will direct you and crown your efforts with success" (TLB). Because I'm stubborn, that kind of surrender usually takes time. Often, it's this place of despair and surrender that God is looking for before He will move ahead and open the door of opportunity for us. When we wait, the dream remains God's dream.

Unfortunately, it's possible to make a dream from God our master rather than God Himself. A dream can actually become the driving force of your life, more important than anything else. Christ reminds

> In everything you do, put God first, and he will direct you and crown your efforts with success.
>
> —Proverbs 3:6, TLB

us of the danger of trying to have two masters: "No one can serve two masters. Either he will hate the one and love the other, or he will be devoted to the one and despise the other" (Matthew 6:24).

So, putting our dream in front of God in our lives will drive us to despise God. More important than pleasing Him, more important than doing things His way, will be the drive to accomplish the dream. We'll despise Him because He's not working on *our* schedule or perhaps even standing in the way.

The crucial skill of waiting settles this issue and helps us put God in the place where He belongs. It restrains us from grasping what isn't ours. The anxiety and disappointment we experience are evidence of the death that is going on in us, the death of our dream and the birth of God's.

Perseverance Removes the Failure Issue

If it's God's dream, then He's responsible for its fulfillment. I'm merely the servant—His tool, His instrument. When we come to realize this, our priorities change. The most important thing is not whether my dream is fulfilled, but rather that I am faithful in pursuing the opportunity and using everything I can to serve God to meet the dream. Don't misunderstand. No emotionally healthy person likes to fail. This attitude doesn't necessarily make failure less painful, but it does ensure that failure is not fatal to us. If this is truly God's dream, ultimately, it's His responsibility to fulfill it.

Far from removing the drive, this kind of commitment to God allows us to throw ourselves into God's will with reckless abandon. We have nothing to lose.

Perseverance at the Outset Ensures Strength in the Stretch

Waiting is a tremendous blessing over the long haul. If the opportunity comes too quickly and easily at first, there's a tremendous temptation down the road, when the adversities do come, to think,

Oh, my goodness, I've walked ahead of God. I've moved out into a place that God doesn't want me to be. Too many Christians try to interpret God's will through their circumstances. However, things going my way doesn't mean I'm doing God's will any more than adversity means I am out of God's will. I'll never forget a Christian in real estate development who justified a lawsuit against fellow Christians—even though the Bible clearly forbids suing other Christians—by saying, "It must be God's will, because God is really blessing my business and family right now." Sometimes, the bills don't come due until the end.

When we wait and watch God's hand obviously moving in the affairs of our lives, removing obstacles we could not move and opening doors of opportunity we could not open, we know that we didn't get into this dream by ourselves. One of the most powerful things we can do when we get discouraged is to remember how God's good hand was upon us in the past. When we can remind ourselves of the remarkable ways we got into this dream in the first place, there's no confusion about why we're here and what we're to be doing. God put us here, like a turtle on a fence post, as a friend of mine likes to say. That turtle didn't get on that fence post by itself; someone put it there. If God put us here, He's still here with us. And that's all that matters, even in the toughest of storms.

Perseverance is sometimes the hardest pill to swallow, but God prescribes it for our spiritual health. God is much more desirous of our success than we are, so if He can wait, so can we.

Proverbs 21:1 reminds us that a king's heart is like a channel of water—the banks of a river or stream direct its path and determine its direction. So God directs the king, the president, the governor, the mayor, the employer, the spouse, the

GrowthOp

Are you tempted to run ahead of God in some area of your life? What do you think He may be trying to teach you?

parent—anyone in authority over us. He can open and close doors any time He wishes.

Waiting Is Not Wasting

Growth Op

While you wait, work on improving your "game." At the beginning of this chapter we saw that Tom Lehman didn't quit. Make a list of skills you might improve on or acquire while you wait for the "main event." Practice them daily.

Also, prayer makes practice perfect in the waiting game. As you wait, remember the most important thing you can do is turn your dream and your waiting over to God on a day-by-day, minute-by-minute basis.

In Nehemiah's case, note God's method of turning a king's heart—through Nehemiah himself, an ordinary man. Men and women are often God's method. God used Nehemiah to turn the heart of the king, and God is still looking for men and women He can use to turn the hearts of kings and leaders and societies and churches and businesses and families. Men and women who prepare themselves, pray, and use every legitimate means to accomplish the dreams God gives them but are willing to wait for His timing. Men and women who are sold out to Jesus Christ and have placed every skill, tool, and opportunity into the hands of the Master, just as Nehemiah did, blending divine and human resources together in a beautiful act of faith.

14

Is Your Vision Contagious?

Where there is no vision,
the people perish.

KING SOLOMON, PROVERBS 29:18, KJV

Today, as in the time of Nehemiah,
the one supreme need is inspiration.

WALTER ADENEY

C

. R. Smith, one of the founders of American Airlines, stopped once in Nashville, Tennessee. He found two desks in the American Airlines sector of the airport. On one a phone was madly ringing. Sitting at the other, with his feet propped up, a man was reading a newspaper. Smith said, "Your phone is ringing." The man said, "That's reservations. I'm maintenance." Smith answered the phone, and it was a father urgently needing to get to California. Smith rattled off the schedule from memory to the man and hung up. The other man, attracted by Smith's knowledge of the schedule, said, "Say, that was pretty good. Do you work for American Airlines?" Smith said, "Yes, I do. And you used to."

The Bible consistently testifies that the Christian life is more than sitting around waiting for heaven to come. God wants to use us — and to do so significantly. The only ability He requires for His service is availability, because the resources and abilities are His. All we need to do is go to work trusting in Him. It's not someone else's job to answer the call — it's our job. The need is not for better men and women, but for men and women God can use. He's not looking for a new generation of heroes, but men and women who trust only in Him.

Nehemiah understood that God's vision for His people was more than just sitting around, and when the phone rang in his ear one day, he picked it up. Because he was available, God spoke to him through his brother Hanani and gave him a dream. We've seen how Nehemiah was able to turn that dream into an opportunity. Because he saw his own limitations so clearly, he prayed fervently to a God who had no limitations. Because he was a servant and knew he didn't have the prerogative to act on his own, he waited for his Master's timing. He waited not only on God, but also for God to move in the king's heart. Because he believed God, he prepared himself — faith begets organization and preparation, not disorder and presumption. When the opportunity came, Nehemiah was ready to walk through the door with a plan. He knew what he needed and he asked for it.

The Next Step

Nehemiah had a dream and God opened the door of opportunity. But that opportunity was still only that — an opportunity. The rubber of desire had still to meet the road of reality. When Nehemiah arrived in Jerusalem,

Have you heard the phone ring lately? What keeps you from answering?

the hard work had only just begun. Nehemiah rolled up his sleeves and began to turn that opportunity into stones and timber.

Our dreams will always involve other people if they're God's dreams, because God's dreams do not involve lone individuals. If the job is God's, it's always bigger than we are, and it always includes others. Other people have roles and parts to play, so it's important that we effectively communicate our dreams to them, that we make our vision *contagious*.

Since Nehemiah's dream involved mobilizing a vast number of volunteers, eliminating the initial inertia and motivating people were absolutely crucial to the fulfillment of his dream.

First Impressions

With politics as nasty as they were in Palestine at the time, it might have been tempting for Nehemiah to sneak into town anonymously. However, Nehemiah arrived with the dignity befitting his office. He moved through the provinces with authority and entered Jerusalem with full military escort and attention. "So I went to the governors of Trans-Euphrates and gave them the king's letters. The king had also sent army officers and cavalry with me" (Nehemiah 2:9).

If first impressions are important, Nehemiah made a good one. He certainly made an impression on his enemies. From the day his foot hit Judean soil, they knew this man was someone they would have to contend with. "When Sanballat the Horonite and Tobiah the Ammonite official heard about this, they were very much disturbed that someone had come to promote the welfare of the Israelites" (2:10).

Sanballat, Tobiah, and Geshem the Arab, whom we'll meet later, were petty potentates who governed small parts of Palestine under Persian rule. As long as Jerusalem lay in ruins, they prospered. With Nehemiah on the scene their scam was about over and they knew it.

Nehemiah also must have made an important impression on the people of Jerusalem as he rode into town. Just as it was displeasing to the enemies of Israel that someone had come on Israel's behalf, it must have been wonderfully assuring to the Jerusalemites and brought them a great deal of joy that someone had arrived to seek the welfare of the sons and daughters of Israel.

Nehemiah did not announce his plans to the city immediately. He wisely arrived without explanation. I would have expected his entry procession into Jerusalem to have wound its way through the narrow streets to one of the plazas, where he would have dismounted and greeted the city dignitaries. There Nehemiah would announce all of his great plans; hand out the trowels, the plumb lines, and the bricks; and proclaim, "We're going to build." In fact, he was there three days before he did anything.

He waited until the proper moment to announce his plans. His enthusiasm for the job ahead was controlled by wisdom. You see, Nehemiah's leadership began with the ear and not the mouth. Far too many seem to have only outgoing communication lines, barraging people with their message. Great leaders, however, are also great listeners.

Before Nehemiah announced his plan for Jerusalem, he needed firsthand knowledge. To get that, he practiced something almost every leader understands. Modern business managers call this "management by walking around," or MBWA.

He needed firsthand information about the political climate. Nehemiah understood that there were significant hostile forces, both within and without the city. The enemies from without worked for the distress, not the prosperity, of the city of Jerusalem. And any of the forces from within—fear, self-doubt, self-depreciation, despair—could sap his strength and destroy his dreams. Nehemiah needed to mingle in the Jewish community and find out for himself the status and morale of his people.

Nehemiah needed to *know* the people—who the leaders were, who was enthusiastic, who was able, who was willing. He realized there was no way he could accomplish his dream alone or even compel others to do the task on his say-so. This dream must be delegated, and other people must be brought into authority as well. J. Oswald Sanders, in his classic book *Spiritual Leadership*, defined leadership like this: "One definition of leadership is the ability to recognize the special abilities and limitations of others, combined with the capacity to fit each one into the job where he will do his best. He who is successful in getting things done through others is exercising the highest type of leadership."[1] A true judge of men, Dwight L. Moody once said he would rather put a thousand men to work than do the work of a thousand men. A true leader has the ability to choose people to whom he or she can safely delegate authority, and then actually delegate it.

Also, before Nehemiah said anything, he needed to know first-hand what shape the walls were in.

> *I went to Jerusalem, and after staying there three days I set out during the night with a few men. I had not told anyone what my God had put in my heart to do for Jerusalem. There were no mounts with me except the one I was riding on.*
>
> *By night I went out through the Valley Gate toward the Jackal Well and the Dung Gate, examining the walls of Jerusalem, which had been broken down, and its gates, which had been destroyed by fire. Then I moved on toward the Fountain Gate and the King's Pool, but there was not enough room for my mount to get through; so I went up the valley by night, examining the wall. Finally, I turned back and reentered through the Valley Gate. The officials did not know where I had gone or what I was doing, because as yet I had said nothing to the Jews or the priests or nobles or officials or any others who would be doing the work. (2:11-16)*

While others slept, Nehemiah—wide-awake, burdened, aware of the desperate need of the city—surveyed the ruins, assessed the situation, and considered the enormous task in front of him. As Nehemiah circled the destruction, I'm sure his heart bled. As he saw the mounds of rock, I'm sure his heart must have trembled a little in fear at the gigantic task ahead. But the time for crying and trembling was past. It was time for action. But what action was appropriate in this situation?

Growth Op

First impressions are so important. What kind of first impression do you make?

It seems likely that Nehemiah was not only assessing the walls, but he was also figuring out his plan of attack. Nehemiah was a good student of human nature. He was waiting for the right psychological moment to make his announcement.

Sharing the Dream

No great dream has ever been brought to reality without someone taking the risk to communicate to other people ideas that might be ridiculed and rejected. This is a key ingredient to the crucial task of sharing the contagion. Whether the leader was Joan of Arc, Winston Churchill, Martin Luther King, Jr., or Lee Iacocca, the dream depended on that leader's ability to communicate well with those he or she wanted to inspire. Whether your dream is large or small, whether it will involve thousands or just a few, your ability to bring other people along with you on your journey toward your dream depends a lot on your ability to communicate the vision to them.

When Nehemiah was thoroughly prepared, he stepped forward to make his announcement. Nehemiah's message was no half-baked pronouncement; it was calculated to do one thing—inspire hope in a defeated people's heart.

A casual piecing together of the times might lead one to believe that those who had returned to Jerusalem were lazy, unmotivated people waiting for someone else to do their work. After all, they had been back ninety years and still had no walls. Similarly, we might assume that the British were unmotivated losers if we had looked only at the early part of World War II. We believe that there are no unmotivated people, just people who haven't listened to the right dreamer.

Following the collapse of France and the evacuation at Dunkirk, it seemed that no one could stop the German forces. England stood alone against Hitler's quest to dominate all of Europe. The Soviet Union had been neutralized by a treaty, and the United States was very reluctant to enter another European conflict. With England ill-prepared and ill-equipped to fight off such an invasion, everyone wondered whether they would surrender. If they tried to resist, military strategists predicted a battle lasting only weeks.

The experts forgot, however, to factor in one potent ingredient. A sixty-five-year-old politician with a checkered political career had just become prime minister of England in May of 1940. On May 13, just before France fell, he gave his first speech as prime minister, saying, "I have nothing to offer but blood, toil, tears, and sweat." He brought one other thing as well—hope. Though surprising, it's not an overestimation to say that England and perhaps the whole Western world owe their freedom to the ability of Winston Churchill to bring hope to a nation that had lost it. As his anxious countrymen listened intently to their radios, Churchill echoed his defiance of tyranny.

The Battle of France is over. I expect the Battle of Britain is about to begin. Upon this battle depends the survival of Christian civilization. . . . The whole fury and might of the enemy must very soon be turned on us. Hitler knows that he will have to break us on this island or lose the war. If we stand up to him, all Europe may be free and the life of the world may move forward into broad sunlit uplands. But if we fail, then the whole world, including the United States, including all that we have known and cared for, will sink into the abyss of a new Dark Age made more sinister, and perhaps more

175

protracted, by the lights of a perverted science. Let us therefore brace ourselves to our duties and so bear ourselves that, if the British Empire and its commonwealth lasts for a thousand years, men will say: "This was their finest hour."²

Inspired by that vision, the British people did rise to their finest hour believing they could resist the enormous force of Hitler's armies. Churchill believed in his country, and he also believed in his people. He believed the British people did not want peace and safety at any price; he believed freedom was dear to them and that they were willing to pay a price for that freedom. He believed they possessed energy and abilities that had not been called forth to that particular point. Through dogged determination and defiance, he galvanized that spirit in the British people.

The power of a man or a woman with a dream has to be one of the most potent forces in all the world. And the crucial ability to share that dream with others, which is the point of this chapter, makes all the difference, not only to the dreamer but perhaps also to the world. Though shorter than Churchill's address, Nehemiah's speech to his fellow Jews was no less packed with hope and motivating power.

Then I said to them, "You see the trouble we are in: Jerusalem lies in ruins, and its gates have been burned with fire. Come, let us rebuild the wall of Jerusalem, and we will no longer be in disgrace." I also told them about the gracious hand of my God upon me and what the king had said to me. (2:17-18)

How to Communicate Your Dream

Let's be clear. You certainly don't need to be an orator like Churchill to communicate your dream, but there are several things about this communication process we can learn from Nehemiah.

Nehemiah spoke to the people personally and directly. He did not depend on someone else to translate his plan. The communication of vision is the sole province of the leader. It's the leader's job to share the vision and to call forth enthusiasm in his listeners. No one else can do this for you.

Nehemiah appealed to their hearts. Educators, leaders, psychologists have all recognized that there are two major types of motivation: *extrinsic motivation*, which is external, materialistic, and coercive in a sense, coming from the outside; and *intrinsic motivation*, which comes from within a person, his or her own desires and needs. Extrinsic motivation can be effective, but it's always temporary. Intrinsic motivation is harder, but it's always stronger and longer lasting. It's not surprising that Nehemiah, like most great leaders, used appeals that hooked the intrinsic desires of his hopeless audience.

The challenge again is not to motivate unmotivated people, but to discover the desires that the Holy Spirit has placed in people's hearts and pour fuel on that fire. To do that the leader must know his or her people.

• •

The best-kept secret in America today is that people would rather work hard for something they believe in than enjoy a pampered idleness.

—JOHN W. GARDNER,
FORMER SECRETARY OF HEALTH, EDUCATION, AND WELFARE

First of all, Nehemiah called on the Jerusalemites to evaluate their situation (2:17). It's possible to live in a mess so long that you actually get used to it. This was certainly the case for the people living in and around Jerusalem. Nehemiah called attention to this; he woke them up. He said, "Look around you. This is not the way it's supposed to be."

• •

The dream begins with a teacher who believes in you, who tugs and pushes you on to the next plateau, sometimes poking you with a sharp stick called truth.

—DAN RATHER

177

Leaders do not pamper people's complacency. They expect the best of those they lead and call them to live up to the potential they know they have. Leaders trust them and treat them with respect, even when they look anything but respectful. They call on ability they know is there, even when the people look like failures.

· ·

We are not what we are, nor do we treat or esteem each other for such, but for what we are capable of being.

—HENRY DAVID THOREAU

Nehemiah appealed to their national pride. He basically said to the people, "Look at us. People see us and they laugh at us—the people of God." Pride is only bad when it's motivated by selfishness. All of us should desire an excellence that pushes past mediocrity and comfort with the status quo. Climbing out of mediocrity requires faith and sacrifice.

Each generation has its examples of those willing to pay the price to change—men and women who thought their dreams were so important that they were willing to sacrifice everything to realize them. Patrick Henry believed a man should be willing to pay whatever freedom cost: "Is life so dear or peace so sweet as to be purchased at the price of chains and slavery? Forbid it, Almighty God. I know not what course others may take, but as for me, give me liberty or give me death."

The fifty-six men who signed the Declaration of Independence and dreamed of what America might be, paid a tremendous price. Of those men, five were captured and tortured by the British before they died; nine died in the war due to bullets or hardships; twelve had their homes sacked, looted, burned, or occupied by the enemy; two lost sons; and one had two sons captured.

There is no security in this world, only opportunity.

—GENERAL DOUGLAS MACARTHUR

Nehemiah challenged the people with an "impossible" task.

There's nothing so compelling as a leader who believes you can do great things. Each of us, deep down inside, knows there is more within than we are called to bring forth in the mundane flow of life. The man or woman who calls us to a task that requires us to be all that we can be taps an energy from God in every person.

- -

A man who has never lost himself in a cause bigger than himself has missed one of life's mountaintop experiences. Only in losing himself does he find himself. Only then does he discover all the latent strengths he never knew he had and which otherwise would have remained dormant.

—RICHARD M. NIXON

We believe that most men and women want to give more to life than they are giving, but they are lacking a cause significant enough to call forth their best. Living in the cocoon is really pretty boring. Let's give them something that calls them out and requires that they be butterflies rather than caterpillars.

- -

Living the good life is frequently dull, flat and commonplace. Our greatest need is to make life fiery, creative, and capable of spiritual struggle.

—NIKOLAI BERDYAEV, RUSSIAN CHRISTIAN PHILOSOPHER (1874–1948)

There is no magic in small plans. When I consider my ministry, I think of the world. Anything less than that would not be worthy of Christ nor His will for my life.

—HENRIETTA MEARS, AUTHOR

The Kind of Dreamer People Follow

But why in the world should the Jews follow Nehemiah? Why should they leave the comfort of their mediocrity and press forward into

Are the size of your dreams worthy of Christ?

this project that no one was really sure could be completed?

Nehemiah identified with their distress. The pronoun *we* is the secret of all leadership. Sure, he was a man of authority, but other authority figures had come and padded their pockets. Here at last was a governor who cared. His sincere words, coupled with his willingness to leave the palace out of a deep concern for them, gave them the confidence to trust him not only as a leader but also as a servant.

• •

People ask the difference between a leader and a boss. . . . The leader works in the open, and the boss in covert. The leader leads, and the boss drives.

—THEODORE ROOSEVELT

There's also one more aspect of Nehemiah's appeal to the people that completes our picture of his motivation of them. He told them his story. "I also told them about the gracious hand of my God upon me and what the king had said to me" (2:18).

Alan Loy McGinnis reminds us of the power of stories. "Stories . . . convince us because they appeal to our hearts rather than our heads. They have the ability to stir our feelings powerfully and to change our attitudes."[3]

Every time Kathy gets behind a microphone, tells her story, and shares her vision that "stronger families build stronger communi-

People read a dream first of all through the leader. What kind of leader do you need to be?

ties; stronger communities build a stronger culture; and a stronger culture builds a stronger country," she gets a loud ovation. People catch her vision that there is hope.

Nehemiah's story not only inspired confidence in his leadership, but it inspired confidence in God as well. His words of encouragement took the focus off the problem and put them on the problem solver. The people heard Nehemiah's story and saw that the impossible dream was possible through the greatness of God. Nehemiah was able to lift their hearts and help them believe that the dream might be feasible.

If you want people to listen to you, if you want people's help in the achievement of your dreams, you must remind them that God is a God of the impossible. Christ said it: "With God, nothing is impossible." The apostle Paul said it: "I can do all things through him who strengthens me." Nehemiah said it in 2:20: "The God of heaven will give us success. We his servants will start rebuilding."

Growth Op

Think of a time you caught someone else's vision. What inspired you? How did you first hear about it? What appealed to you? What made you think the impossible was possible?

> *If you would win a man to your cause, first convince him that you are his sincere friend. Therein is a drop of honey that catches his heart, which, say what you will, is the great high-road to his reason, and which, when once gained, you will find but little trouble in convincing his judgment of the justice of your cause.*[4]

The Response of the People

How did the people respond to Nehemiah? How did they respond to his appeal? How did they respond to his dream? Chapter 2 verse 18 tells us, "They replied, 'Let us start rebuilding.' So they began this good work."

15

Facing the Critics

No great movement designed to change the world can bear to be laughed at or belittled. Mockery is a rust that corrodes all it touches.

MILAN KUNDERA, CZECHOSLOVAKIAN AUTHOR (B. 1929)

I find the pain of a little censure, even when it is unfounded, is more acute than the pleasure of much praise.

THOMAS JEFFERSON

Everybody has at least one. It may be your mother, mother-in-law, father, brother, spouse, boss, coworker — somebody who, in your mind, has the personality of a yard dog. Unfortunately, some people in the world get a kick out of making cynical remarks, cutting comments, and critical evaluations. They seem to relish watching our countenance drop, our smile dissolve, and our energy dissipate. In all fairness, many times it seems these people don't really mean to be dream-killing critics. They just live in a very small world and have a hard time seeing outside its boundaries. It's dangerous out there, and they don't want us to get hurt. They can't imagine how anyone would want to color outside the lines, do something avant-garde, change the status quo, be a maverick or a pioneer. On the other hand, there are people who purposefully try to kill others' dreams. Maybe they're jealous because they don't have the courage to step out on their own dreams. Maybe they're scared our dream will upset their comfortable world. Maybe they're getting even because someone squelched their own dream.

There's no getting around it. If you dream, and especially when you see your dream becoming a reality, you can expect to be attacked. The fact is, *there is no opportunity without opposition.* But men and women who turn dreams into reality must have the ability to see through the criticism to its reality, accepting what's helpful and rejecting what's not. There's a fine line between holding on to the courage of your convictions and thinking you are beyond reproach. No matter how successful we become or how insulated success makes us, we all need accountability. We must learn to deal with criticism. If we fail to listen to our critics, chances are we'll fail to deal with the character traits that will keep us ultimately from success.

Some years ago, when I read David's imprecatory psalms, I wondered what it would be like to have a real enemy who was out for my blood. Oh, I had experienced my share of spats, but no full-blown warfare with someone chasing me with a spear or hating my guts. Ironically, I finally had that experience — the hating of my guts, that is—when I helped start a church, of all things. Real dreams provoked real conflict.

I'll have to admit, I did have grand dreams. I dreamed of a church that brought a positive message of grace and biblical Christianity to a town that had rarely seen such. I dreamed of a church that reached out and led countless people to Christ; a church with authentic relationships; a church that had an impact on the entire community, not just a holy huddle.

After four years of pursuing this dream, I came to grips with three things. First, as a friend of mine says, the greatest myth in America is that churches want to grow. Second, the term *grace*, to some people, means license—license to control other people's behavior, rather than helping them grow. Third, people who are highly developmental (like me) rather than maintenance-oriented, will be under constant suspicion as to their motives for pushing the church to reach out to others.

Unfortunately, by the time I figured this out, I had accumulated an enemy or two. It's hard to forget the acidic attack of one of the church leaders over lunch one day. He told me that my ministry was worthless, my motives impure, and my walk with Christ nonexistent. Then, to ice the cake, he added, "Maybe you could have a ministry in another church." (And he named a denomination he held in utter contempt.) As I walked away from lunch that day, I thought, *Now I know what it's like to have an enemy.* I think I experienced that day at least a little of what Nehemiah must have felt.

> All cruel people describe themselves as paragons of frankness!
>
> —Tennessee Williams

Sanballat's Psychological Warfare

The battle of words that began when Nehemiah arrived in Jerusalem continued with ferocity when real progress on the wall was observable. The reaction of Sanballat and his Palestinian alliance was no surprise. They were furious.

When Sanballat heard that we were rebuilding the wall, he became angry and was greatly incensed. He ridiculed the Jews, and in the presence of his associates and the army of Samaria, he said, "What are those feeble Jews doing? Will they restore their wall? Will they offer sacrifices? Will they finish in a day? Can they bring the stones back to life from those heaps of rubble — burned as they are?"

Tobiah the Ammonite, who was at his side, said, "What they are building — if even a fox climbed up on it, he would break down their wall of stones!" (Nehemiah 4:1-3)

The vision of the future that Sanballat and company saw as they looked at the half-repaired walls was no dream. To them, it was a nightmare. Their fragile hold on Jerusalem loosened with every stone that was put in place. As is typical with insecure people, they would not surrender power or influence without a fight. Their first line of defense was caustic criticism calculated to demoralize Nehemiah and the builders, weaken their resolve, and destroy their hope. The naysayers belittled their ability, questioned their motives, ridiculed their enthusiasm, questioned their grip on reality, and denigrated their work.

• •

The effect of criticism is a dividing up of the powers of the one criticized; the Holy Ghost is the only One in the true position to criticize, He alone is able to show what is wrong without hurting and wounding.

—OSWALD SANDERS, *SPIRITUAL LEADERSHIP*

Things haven't changed much in twenty-five centuries. Criticism, mockery, and cynicism are weapons in the arsenal of small people who must attack others to maintain some degree of personal equilibrium.

*A person who sees no heroism in himself can general-
ize and decide that there is no such thing as a hero.
There'd better be no such thing, because such people
gave up trying to be heroic long ago; now they can't look
up without being reminded how far down they are.*[1]

Growth Op

With criticism, as with almost everything in life, reading Scripture helps put things in perspective. When you've been criticized, keep these proverbs in mind:

To reject criticism is to harm yourself and your own best
interests. (Proverbs 15:32, TLB)

A rebuke impresses a man of discernment
more than a hundred lashes a fool. (17:10)

A man of knowledge uses words with restraint,
and a man of understanding is even-tempered. (17:27)

A fool finds no pleasure in understanding
but delights in airing his own opinions. (18:2)

He who answers before listening—
that is his folly and his shame. (18:13)

It is a badge of honor to accept valid criticism. (25:12, TLB)

A man who refuses to admit his mistakes can never be successful. But if he confesses and forsakes them, he gets
another chance. (28:13, TLB)

Nehemiah's Response

Responding to criticism is the key point of this chapter, so we must
ask: How does a visionary like Nehemiah respond to a verbal attack?

It would have seemed natural for this tough-minded dreamer to retaliate and bite back. Surprisingly, he didn't engage his critics. But neither did he bottle up his anger. He took the matter to the only One who could do anything about the situation. Nehemiah prayed. He recognized that there was more going on here than two strong leaders with differing views about the future squaring off for a verbal duel. There was spiritual warfare going on, and it's important to understand that if we are involved in God's cause, we can expect the same. Confronted with a spiritual threat, Nehemiah went directly to his Commander in Chief.

> *Hear us, O our God, for we are despised. Turn their insults back on their own heads. Give them over as plunder in a land of captivity. Do not cover up their guilt or blot out their sins from your sight, for they have thrown insults in the face of the builders. (Nehemiah 4:4-5)*

But what should we say about Nehemiah's request? How does this square with Jesus' command in the Gospels: "You have heard that it was said, 'Love your neighbor and hate your enemy.' But I tell you: 'Love your enemies and pray for those who persecute you'" (Matthew 5:43-44)?

I don't think Nehemiah's prayer was what Jesus had in mind when He said, "Pray for those who persecute you." But there are three things that help us understand Nehemiah's prayer. First, this is a national prayer, not a request for personal revenge. Second, God had promised special judgment on those who hindered His people. And third, God's honor was at stake. Mockery of God's people and God's city was an open challenge to God Himself.

Nehemiah not only prayed, he persisted. He kept on going. He wasn't sidetracked in defending himself, derailed in self-pity, or preoccupied with a fight. He sought God and kept his focus on the task at hand.

As a result of Nehemiah's prayer and persistence, the people of Jerusalem stayed on task. Up to this point, the Jews had been an easy mark for ridicule. Under Samaritan domination for years, they were a people without power or champion until Nehemiah showed up. Without his faith and resolve, their determination would have easily turned to despair. His faith renewed their courage. His perspective focused their attention on their Maker, not their mocker.

> Our strength often increases in proportion to the obstacles imposed upon it.
>
> —PAUL DE RAPIN

"So we rebuilt the wall till all of it reached half its height, for the people worked with all their heart" (Nehemiah 4:6).

Facing Criticism

Every dreamer must learn to live with criticism. If we're going to dream and see our dreams become reality, we must develop the ability to measure a critic's value, assess our motives, and wisely determine how to respond properly, or in some cases, not respond. Nehemiah gives us a good strategy to follow.

1. Express your feelings first to God, not men. The apostle Paul reminds us that when we're under stress, the first place to go is to God: "Do not be anxious about anything, but in everything, by prayer and petition, with thanksgiving, present your requests to God" (Philippians 4:6).

2. Stay at your task. One of the marks of godly men is that they are not sidetracked by criticism or attack. They pray, but they don't stop everything to pray. When a fire broke out on D. L. Moody's ship crossing the Atlantic, a friend said, "Mr. Moody, let us go to the other end of the ship and pray." Moody replied, "No sir; we stand right here and pass the buckets and pray hard all the time."[2]

3. Determine the proper response. Should you keep things between you and God? Should you speak up? Should you confess? Before we say anything to anyone, we should evaluate what we intend to say by the standard of God's Word. Paul tells us,

> *Do not let any unwholesome talk come out of your mouths, but only what is helpful for building others up*

HEART measuring stick

according to their needs, that it may benefit those who listen. And do not grieve the Holy Spirit of God, with whom you were sealed for the day of redemption. Get rid of all bitterness, rage and anger, brawling and slander, along with every form of malice. Be kind and compassionate to one another, forgiving each other, just as in Christ God forgave you. (Ephesians 4:29-32)

If we have malice in our hearts, we'd best keep quiet and keep talking to God. Otherwise, our critics will lead us to wallow in their polluted pigsty of hate. Before a word leaves our lips, we should ask, "Will what I want to say help or hinder the person?" If we're not sure, our best option is silence.

• •

I have oft regretted my speech—never my silence.

—PUBLILIUS SYRUS, ROMAN POET (FIRST CENTURY B.C.)

Do you see a man who speaks in haste?
    There is more hope for a fool than for him.

—PROVERBS 29:20

4. Evaluate the truth of what is said. Criticism calls us to make an evaluation. Whatever the source, whatever the motive, there may be some truth in harsh words. Sometimes God sends His messages to us in strange packages. Winston Churchill put it well: "The greatest lesson in life is to know that even fools can be right sometimes."

Let's be honest. None of us has totally pure motives. There is always room for improvement in what we are doing. Rather than wanting no critics, we should welcome their challenge. And I'm afraid we should admit that sometimes we need them to keep us honest.

If our critics are wrong, our integrity will speak for itself. If there is a cor-

• •

The trouble with most of us is that we would rather be ruined by praise than saved by criticism.

—NORMAN VINCENT PEALE

190

rection to be made, we need to admit it, make it right, and thank God that He has called it to our attention now rather than later. We must be careful never to put ourselves in a position where we can't learn from our worst enemy. We should never be afraid of the truth, no matter how painful. It sets us free.

5. *Don't concern yourself with your critics' motives.* If critics tell you they are only trying to help, there is really no way for you to know for sure. It's a waste of time and not your concern anyway. Your concern is the accuracy of the criticism and your own motives.

A story is told of General Robert E. Lee in which he spoke with the highest regard to President Davis about a certain officer. Upon hearing this, another officer standing next to him said, "General, do you know that the man of whom you speak so highly to the President is one of your bitterest enemies, and misses no opportunity to malign you?"

"Yes," replied General Lee, "but the President asked my opinion of him; he did not ask for his opinion of me."

The lesson here is, don't descend to the level of your critic — since you really don't know his or her motives — and keep your own motives pure.

6. *Let the quality of your work and character speak for itself.* If you are attacked personally, defending yourself will be of little value. Let the quality of your work and character speak for you. The worst thing that could happen is being dragged into a verbal fistfight. It will distract you and make you a deserving target for critical people.

> When your work speaks for itself, don't interrupt.
>
> HENRY J. KAISER, AMERICAN INDUSTRIALIST (1882–1967)

7. *Keep your eyes on Jesus.* Focus on God's ability, not your circumstances. He is the source of your strength and identity. If you lose sight of Him, you've lost.

> Our ability to act well "when the time comes" depends partly, perhaps largely, upon the quality of our habitual objects of attention.
>
> —IRIS MURDOCH, ENGLISH NOVELIST AND PHILOSOPHER (B. 1919)

This chapter has dealt with the important art of facing our critics. Here are seven tips that will help you do just that as you pursue your dream:

1. First, stop what you're doing and look directly into the eyes of your critic and actively listen to what he or she is saying. If you're on the phone, tell the person that you are listening. Don't interrupt. Let your critic talk.

2. Try to listen in between the lines—discern what is going on behind the remarks. It could be that you are the object of someone's pent-up frustration or hormones, with nothing personal intended. "He who answers a matter before he hears the facts, it is folly and shame to him" (Proverbs 18:13, AMP).

3. Realize and accept that the criticism is the other person's perspective, which he or she believes to be correct. Therefore, it doesn't do any good to accuse the critic of being oversensitive or irrational. If the criticism is exaggerated, don't get hung up trying to correct him or her on the spot.

4. Don't evade the issue or bring up another topic. Deal with it.

5. Don't make fun of the criticism, as it may be a sensitive issue from the critic's perspective. You may be perceived as sarcastic and belittling.

6. Try to remain open and find truth in the criticism. Nobody's perfect. There is usually something valid, even if it's poppy-seed size, to the critic's words.

7. After you've listened to the criticism, ask for an opportunity to respond. Begin by restating what you heard the critic saying to make sure you understood. Then, share what you feel about the criticism and what you believe to be true. Admit what you think is correct about the criticism. Share your thoughts and feelings in a controlled manner.

16

Dealing with Discouragement

If all difficulties were known at the outset of a long journey, most of us would never start out at all.

DAN RATHER

And let us not get tired of doing what is right, for after a while we will reap a harvest of blessing if we don't get discouraged and give up.

THE APOSTLE PAUL, GALATIANS 6:9, TLB

"We are not quitters." My father said those words to me over and over when I was a young girl. They were woven through the tapestry of my childhood and adolescence. "I want to quit piano lessons," I complained. Or "I'm afraid I'm going to fail this Latin class—I want to get out before I do" or "I want to drop out of college."

But his response was always, "In our family, we are not quitters." You see, my father has always believed that if something is worth having, it's worth hanging in there for. Life is hard, but you can't let the hard things get you down. When something bad happens, there's always a corresponding good attitude or action you can take—if you choose to. This philosophy has always made up the fiber of his being—even as he has had to endure many hardships as he's grown older.

On one particular family trip to visit my parents when our boys were younger, John, Joel, and I were playing spades with my dad at the kitchen table. Out of the blue, for the first time, Joel noticed my dad's partially crippled hands. From childlike curiosity, he asked, "Granddaddy, what's wrong with your hands?"

My dad smiled and answered, "Oh, that's just my arthritis." He held out one hand and continued, "Even though these three fingers won't move, I've still got two that work fine." He wiggled the two fingers he was holding his cards between.

I've seen this same find-the-positive-in-the-negative attitude when people have tried to discourage him, when his business has "gone south," as he says, when the circumstances of his life—whatever they be—have been anything but easy.

He set a wonderful example. He taught me to pick myself up and dust myself off when things go wrong, when things get hard, and adjust my dreams a little—but never, never to quit if I'm pursuing something worthy. This is something very precious. It's sort of a stick-to-itiveness that now permeates every fiber of my being. It's really hard for me to give something up or to quit.

But even though I'm wired like this, it's still easy to get down.

It's easy to get discouraged, frustrated, and to feel lonely — wanting desperately for someone to cheer me on in the midst of a hard endeavor, wishing things could be easier, craving some kind of a break that would make a dream I'm pursuing come true overnight.

We live in a complex, imperfect, sinful world. Sometimes it's hard enough to get through the everyday problems, let alone dream about making a difference in the grand scheme of God's universe. And that's exactly how Satan would want us to feel so God's plans for His world will not come to be.

It's probably safe to say that Nehemiah had some down days too — plenty of them, in fact. Since he was human, we can assume that he got tired, frustrated, and discouraged. There were probably days when he wondered if he could go on. And it's encouraging to know that people of faith like Nehemiah faced the same kind of discouraging circumstances we encounter without throwing in the towel — or the *trowel* in Nehemiah's case.

> God has no problems, only plans.
> —CORRIE TEN BOOM

A Tough Day on the Walls

If you believe that obeying God and doing His will somehow ensure smooth sailing for your dreams, a quick read of Nehemiah 4 will cure that delusion. A trouble-free existence is a dream that won't happen for any of us this side of heaven, any more than it did for Nehemiah.

> *So we rebuilt the wall till all of it reached half its height, for the people worked with all their heart.*
> *But when Sanballat, Tobiah, the Arabs, the Ammonites and the men of Ashdod heard that the repairs to Jerusalem's walls had gone ahead and that the gaps were being closed, they were very angry. They all plotted together to come and fight against Jerusalem and stir up trouble against it. But we prayed to our God and*

posted a guard day and night to meet this threat.

Meanwhile, the people in Judah said, "The strength of the laborers is giving out, and there is so much rubble that we cannot rebuild the wall."

Also our enemies said, "Before they know it or see us, we will be right there among them and will kill them and put an end to the work."

Then the Jews who lived near them came and told us ten times over, "Wherever you turn, they will attack us."

Therefore I stationed some of the people behind the lowest points of the wall at the exposed places, posting them by families, with their swords, spears and bows. After I looked things over, I stood up and said to the nobles, the officials and the rest of the people, "Don't be afraid of them. Remember the Lord, who is great and awesome, and fight for your brothers, your sons and your daughters, your wives and your homes." (Nehemiah 4:6-14)

Even though Nehemiah was halfway to his dream, he wasn't halfway through his problems. They were just beginning.

The Threat Outside the Walls

Their strategy of ridicule and mockery having failed, the Palestinian alliance reconvened to discuss an escalation of their resistance. Putting their heads together, they came up with a new strategy — threat of open attack. They didn't want a full-scale war, they just wanted to cause enough disturbance to disrupt the work. It was an excellent economic strategy that, given the situation in Jerusalem, had a high likelihood of working. How could Nehemiah possibly field a defense and man the work force at the same time?

The pressure was just enough to turn the tide of morale in Jerusalem. The threat of doom and despair loomed on the horizon. But things were only going to get worse, because there was another threat.

The Threat Within the Walls

Men and women neck-deep in rubble hit the wall, so to speak, emotionally. The long hours, psychological pressure, and now the reduction in the work force necessitated by guard duty began to take its toll. The people were overwhelmed. They had entered this project with a high level of enthusiasm and zeal. But enthusiasm will only take you so far. They believed that God had led Nehemiah to Jerusalem, they saw his faith and believed that the walls could be rebuilt. But initial drive and excitement had only taken them as far as it could, which, significantly, is always the case.

Whether it's a dream, career, marriage, or even life itself, halfway through is always the toughest place to be and will almost always bring a crisis. Human energy will only take us so far; and when we find ourselves disappointingly short of our goals, and we're not sure we have the resources or energy to finish the job, discouragement can win the day. The temptation is to quit and find something to relieve the pain of failure.

Under the weight of their fatigue, the Jews looked up at the huge piles of debris created by the removal of thousands of limestone blocks made useless by fire. They looked at the task ahead, which must now be accomplished under threat of attack. With past failures coloring their perspective, they didn't think they could go on.

> To tend, unfailingly, unflinchingly, towards a goal, is the secret of success.
>
> —ANNA PAVLOVA, RUSSIAN BALLERINA (1882–1931)

Fear of Failure

I haven't met a person yet who doesn't face discouragement. Everyone has problems. We don't live in a perfect world. In our own lives we've identified major causes of discouragement that threaten to kill our dreams over and over again. First, we fear failure. Fear very well may be the most destructive force in the world. It cripples motivation; destroys enthusiasm; takes away our ability to love;

promotes worry, doubt, and feelings of inadequacy and failure; and robs us of our dreams. It's interesting. Job was right—people fail because they expect to. "What I always feared has happened to me" (Job 3:25, TLB).

Over and over, historians, psychologists, and theologians have told us we become how we see ourselves in our minds. Solomon wrote in Proverbs 23:7: "As he thinketh in his heart, so is he" (KJV).

> God hath not given us the spirit of fear; but of power, and of love, and of a sound mind
>
> —2 TIMOTHY 1:7, KJV

What this means to a dreamer is this: If I harbor fear and think, *I'm afraid I'll be a failure; this dream will never come true*, chances are it won't. An interesting story brought this truth to light for us.

After fifty-seven years on the high wire, Karl Wallenda fell to his death at age seventy-three. In an interview, his wife discussed his last and fatal walk. She said that for three straight months prior to this walk, all Wallenda thought about was falling. This was the first time he had even entertained the thought of falling, she said. He put all his energies into fear of falling, rather than into walking the tightrope. What he feared came to pass.

Evidently God understood from the beginning that fear would be a big problem for humankind. Why else would He have put approximately 350 passages in the Bible that tell us to "fear not"?

Actually, from our limited perspective, there are many fearful aspects about dreaming. Our standard of living may change, other people may be affected, our bank account may shrink. But to my knowledge, worrying about what

Growth Op

List the fears that plague you, then think about their flip (and realistic) side. For example, "I fear failure." The flip side here would be, "I am an imperfect human being who will fail sometimes. But when I do, God is always with me, and He never loves me any less because I fail." Or "People will think I look silly if I try and fail." Flip side: "What will God think if I don't try?" Or "I'll hate myself if I try and fail." Flip side: "God will always love me."

could go wrong or how we might fail *never* helps. Instead of being fearful, we should relax and take our cues from the One who gave us the dream in the first place. Then we have nothing to fear. The dream becomes an exciting adventure—a gift from our Creator.

Victim Mentality

The second major cause of discouragement that threatens to kill our dreams is our circumstances—the ups and downs of human existence.

Our society has adopted a victim mentality about life—"If only I were younger, older, smarter, richer . . . then I could pursue my dream, then I could succeed." We blame our age, health, financial circumstances, peers, spouse, handicaps, and if we are honest, even God for our not fulfilling our dreams. What we're really saying, even if it's under our breath, is, "Poor me, I don't deserve this."

Lord Byron and John Keats, two of the most respected poets of all time, had a clubfoot and tuberculosis, respectively. Certainly they could have embraced a victim mentality, but they didn't. William Gladstone, at the age of eighty, could have said, "Poor me, I'm too old to be elected to a government position." Instead, he became prime minister of Great Britain. J. P. Morgan could have used age as an excuse to slow down. He didn't become a financial giant until after he was sixty years old. John Milton could have felt sorry for himself when he went blind. Instead, he wrote *Paradise Lost*. Harry Truman could have felt slighted because he was not accepted at West Point. He became president.

George Eliot (real name Mary Ann Evans) was over forty when she published her first novel. English novelist Dorothy Sayers wrote several books on God and spirituality while supporting a child she had out of wedlock. Thomas Edison's teacher told his mother that her son was "too dumb to learn." Obviously, he either didn't hear the remark or didn't choose to believe it. Mark Twain didn't wallow in self-pity even though he lived a life of poverty—he became one of our nation's greatest humorists. Franklin D. Roosevelt had polio and was president. After a stroke, Louis Pasteur discovered pasteurization. When Handel wrote the *Messiah*, he was paralyzed and threatened with debtor's prison.

Harlan Sanders, better known as Colonel Sanders, had much he could have been discouraged about. His father died when he was five years old. He quit school at sixteen, and by seventeen he'd already lost four jobs. He was married at eighteen and a father before he was nineteen. When he was twenty his wife left him and took their baby daughter with her. Between the ages of eighteen and twenty-two he failed as a railroad conductor, washed out of the army, flopped as a farmer, was rejected from law school, and bombed as an insurance salesman. He figured he was a pretty good cook, though, so he got a job as a cook and dishwasher in a small cafe.

Eventually he convinced his wife to return home and together they worked in the cafe, cooking and washing dishes, until he retired at age sixty-five. On his first day of retirement he went to the post office and picked up his first Social Security check for $105. He didn't want the government to take care of him and he contemplated suicide.

He decided to write his last will and testament, but instead, he found himself, for the very first time in his life, writing down what he should be and what he would like to do with his remaining years. He decided that he wasn't through yet! There *was* something he could do that no one else he knew could do as well. He knew how to cook!

He went to the bank in his hometown and borrowed $87 against his next Social Security check. With that $87 he bought some boxes and some chicken. Then he went home and fried the chicken in a special recipe he'd developed over the years in that little cafe. He started selling his chicken door-to-door in his hometown of Corbin, Kentucky, and became the king of the Kentucky Fried Chicken empire.

Most likely, at one time or another, all of us have dealt with discouragement in the form of circumstances that hinder or oppose something we dream about doing. Our attitude deteriorates. Our vision blurs. Our courage wanes. While in such a negative mind-set, we're prone to feel overwhelmed about one or more areas of our life and our mind blows things even more out of proportion. We focus on our liabilities, some of which are real but greatly exaggerated, and some of which are imagined. What we must do instead is choose (which is the operative word here, because we do have a choice) to focus on our assets—what we *do* have and what we *can* do—even if it's only something small to begin with. We must not give in to self-pity.

God tells us the source of this kind of attitude in Matthew 16:21-23:

> *From that time on Jesus began to explain to his disciples that he must go to Jerusalem and suffer many things at the hands of the elders, chief priests and teachers of the law, and that he must be killed and on the third day be raised to life.*
>
> *Peter took him aside and began to rebuke him. "Never, Lord!" he said. "This shall never happen to you!"*
>
> *Jesus turned and said to Peter, "Get behind me, Satan! You are a stumbling block to me; you do not have in mind the things of God, but the things of men."*

What if Jesus had answered, "You're right, Peter! I don't deserve to die. After all, I've lived a pretty good life. As a matter of fact, I've lived a perfect life. I deserve better than this!" We might all be tempted to answer like this.

But no, not Jesus. He didn't allow Himself to think like a victim and feel sorry for Himself. Instead, He pointed out the source of this kind of thinking: Satan.

Growth Op

Have you been thinking like a victim? Pick out a situation in your life when you think you failed because somebody else treated you wrongly. Now rewrite the "story." Tell yourself what responsibility you had. Is there something you didn't do but could have that would have changed the outcome? Is bearing a grudge against your victimizer preventing you from getting on with your dream?

Winning over Discouragement

When we get discouraged, we lose the ability to think rationally about the situation. Our response instead is:

➠ I just can't go on.

➠ I (or another person) will never change.

➠ I just don't have the strength.

➠ There's just more than I can do.

➠ I can't do it anymore.

➠ I'm at the end of my rope!

Notice anything significant about these statements or the Jews' lament in Nehemiah? Where's the focus? On self and circumstances.

> Things do not change; we change.
> —HENRY DAVID THOREAU

It's an interesting thing, the human mind. It can only focus on a couple of things at a time. When we're preoccupied with a problem and focus on our own inadequacy to handle it, there's really no room to add God to the picture. The ability to think rationally returns only when we refocus on God's adequacy.

That's the first thing Nehemiah helped his discouraged builders do. He reports, "We prayed." Discouragement is a spiritual battle to be fought with spiritual weapons, and prayer is always our first line of defense. Notice that this time everyone prayed, not just Nehemiah. It's no good just to have someone pray for us. If we want perspective rather than panic, we must focus on God ourselves.

> Trust God and keep your powder dry.
> —OLIVER CROMWELL (1595–1638)

Sometimes our battles contain physical aspects as well. This was certainly true for Nehemiah. Action, as well as prayer, was called for. We can't do much until we pray, but there is almost always something we can do besides prayer. That's not lack of faith. That's wise living.

Wise men and women know that they must act responsibly with the resources and abilities God has given them and trust God at the same time. Prayer without precaution on Nehemiah's part would have been presumption. Precaution without prayer would have been pride. Over and over we see this beautiful balance in his life of human responsibility and confidence in God's sovereignty. So Nehemiah tells us, "We prayed and set up a guard." If you read chapter 4 in its entirety, you'll see that Nehemiah totally reorganized the work. He set up a full-time guard, armed all the workers, and established a defensive strategy in the event of an attack. But look at the cornerstone of his defense tactics and confidence: "At whatever place you hear the sound of the trumpet, rally to us there. Our God will fight for us" (Nehemiah 4:20, NASB).

Nehemiah called the people to pray, he took precaution against attack, but he also called them to remember. "Don't be afraid of them. Remember the Lord, who is great and awesome, and fight for your brothers, your sons and your daughters, your wives and your homes" (4:14).

If those words don't ring a bell for you, think back a few chapters. "Great and awesome" are the same attributes of God that led Nehemiah to pray for Jerusalem when he first heard the news about the walls. The great and awesome God who delivered the Jews from Egypt and brought them to the Promised Land; the great and awesome God who sent them into exile and delivered them back to Jerusalem; the great and awesome God who had answered Nehemiah's prayer and had given them such a good beginning on the walls—this is the same great and awesome God who would fight for them and see this project through.

> If God is for us, who can be against us?
>
> —THE APOSTLE PAUL, ROMANS 8:31

What We Need to Remember

The Hebrew word Nehemiah used that we translate "remember" not only tells us to recall or bring to mind, but to respond to the facts: in this case to celebrate the goodness of God. To remember the Lord is not just to rehearse a cold grocery list of God's deeds, but to take them to heart, to rejoice over them, and to be thankful for His faithfulness—in short, to let Him fill our mind. When we do that, discouragement has nowhere to go but out the window.

With all our focus on the future, it's important to take time to talk about and learn from the past. Remembering is one of the most important antidotes to discouragement we can take, and it is important for at least four reasons.

First, it is commanded by God. David knew this and commanded himself to remember.

> *Praise the LORD, O my soul;*
> *all my inmost being, praise his holy name.*
> *Praise the LORD, O my soul;*
> *and forget not all his benefits. (Psalm 103:1-2)*

When we obey God by taking time to remember what He has done for us, we become men and women filled with gratitude, who want to be more obedient even when things don't go our way. When we take time to remember who we were apart from Christ, and who we are now in God's family (Ephesians 2:11-22), we know where our allegiance lies.

Second, forgetting the Lord is dangerous to your health. Nehemiah knew that the failure to remember had brought about God's judgment.

> *They refused to listen and failed to* remember *the miracles you performed among them. They became stiffnecked and in their rebellion appointed a leader in order to return to their slavery. But you are a forgiving God, gracious and compassionate, slow to anger and abounding in love. Therefore you did not desert them. (Nehemiah 9:17,* emphasis added*)*

When we fail to remember we lose perspective. The danger is not just God's direct judgment, but that we forget where life really is—only in God. Our frantic searches for meaning and acceptance are destined to end in more emptiness and eventually disaster until we turn back to Him.

Third, remembering reminds us of who God is in a time of trouble. Looking out over a fallen, burning Jerusalem, Jeremiah wept and remembered.

> *Yet this I call to mind*
> *and therefore I have hope:*
>
> *Because of the LORD's great love we are not consumed,*
> *for his compassions never fail.*
> *They are new every morning;*
> *great is your faithfulness. (Lamentations 3:21-23)*

During even the darkest time, remembering God's faithfulness reminds us how safe and secure we are right now. Remembering creates a storehouse of mental capital we can draw on in present difficulty, giving us hope for the future when there is nothing left around us in the world to give us hope.

Fourth, in a time of prosperity, remembering reminds us of who we are—that we're not the big shots we may think we are. Moses warned the Jews about pride before they entered the Promised Land.

> *Be careful that you do not forget the LORD your God. . . .*
> *Otherwise, when you eat and are satisfied, when you*
> *build fine houses and settle down, and when your herds*
> *and flocks grow large and your silver and gold increase*
> *and all you have is multiplied, then your heart will*
> *become proud and you will forget the LORD your God,*
> *who brought you out of Egypt, out of the land of slav-*
> *ery. . . . But remember the LORD your God, for it is he*
> *who gives you the ability to produce wealth, and so con-*
> *firms his covenant, which he swore to your forefathers,*
> *as it is today. (Deuteronomy 8:11-14,18)*

> If you want a place in the sun, you have to put up with a few resistors.
>
> —ABIGAIL VAN BUREN

Remembering puts us in our place. All that we have came from God—not from our intelligence, hard work, business savvy, or natural abilities. I've been given everything I have, so the only proper attitude is thanksgiving.

What were the results in Jerusalem? "When our enemies heard that we were aware of their plot and that God had frustrated it, we all returned to the wall, each to his own work" (Nehemiah 4:15).

Nehemiah remembered God, and he called his fellow countrymen to do the same. When they did, discouragement evaporated like the phantom obstacle it is and everyone went back to work with a new zeal to tackle the last half of the job.

Growth Op

Pick one or two older people in your family or church you respect and interview them about what they—or their parents—did when things got tough.

17

Building on the Ashes: When Dreams Die

He who has never failed somewhere, that man cannot be great. Failure is the true test of greatness.

F. D. MATTIESEN, AMERICAN POET

If you want to double your success rate, double your failure rate.

THOMAS WATSON, FOUNDER OF IBM

Men and women who have a continuing impact on culture seem to have one thing in common: They don't believe there's such a thing as failure. It isn't even a word in their vocabulary. Instead they use words like *slip-up, setback, glitch,* or *mistake.* When they do mention the word *failure,* it's almost always in a positive light.

> Failure is only the opportunity to begin again more intelligently.
>
> —HENRY FORD

Thomas Watson, founder of IBM, was legendary for his ability to turn a serious mistake into a learning situation. On one occasion a young executive lost $10 million in a risky venture. When Watson called him in, the executive expected the worst, blurting out, "I guess you want my resignation." Watson replied, "You can't be serious. We've just spent $10 million educating you!"

Whatever we might say positively, failure is never something we strive for. And when it comes, it's never easy. When a dream dies, part of our soul dies as well. For whatever reason our dream died—

> A mistake at least proves that somebody stopped talking long enough to do something.
>
> —*APPLES OF GOLD*

circumstances beyond our control, our own fault, or a combination of causes—life is not over. Failure is never final. A chapter in the book of our life has closed—with a sad ending—but the story continues. If we're still alive, there's still hope. It's always too soon to give up. There's always another chapter to write. Consider the chapters in this man's life.

1. He failed in business at age twenty-two.
2. He was defeated for state legislature at twenty-three.
3. He failed in business again at twenty-four.
4. He was elected to the legislature at twenty-five.
5. His fiancée died when he was twenty-six.
6. He had a nervous breakdown at twenty-seven.
7. He was defeated for Speaker of the House at twenty-nine.

8. He was defeated for elector at thirty-one.
9. His young son died when he was forty-one.
10. He was defeated for the U.S. Senate at forty-six.
11. He was defeated for vice president at forty-seven.
12. He was defeated for the Senate again at forty-nine.

It's painful to read this story, isn't it? By the time I get to chapter 9, I'm tempted to tell this guy, "Give up. Life's not fair. Look, quit trying to be something you're not. Just go back home, quietly practice law, and quit beating yourself up."

Pick a place. Anywhere along the way, he looks like a failure in life. We would never call him that, however, because of the last chapter of his life.

13. He was elected president of the United States at age fifty-one.

What if he had decided, after chapter 1, 5, or even 12, that his life was over? The name Abraham Lincoln would draw a blank from us.

• •

Those who believe they believe in God but without passion in the heart, without anguish of mind, without uncertainty, without doubt, and even at times without despair, believe only in the idea of God, and not in God himself.

—MADELINE L'ENGLE, AMERICAN AUTHOR

What to Do When You've Lost Your Dream

Remember Who God Is

Whatever our situation in life, the most important thing about life is not who we are or even what we've done, but who God is and what He's done. If life depended on us, I'd say "give up." But if it depends on God, there is always hope. Men and women have shown consistently that we can take the most wonderful situations and turn them into living hell. On the other hand, God has proved that He can take the most desperate situations and the most weak or dastardly people and make something wonderful happen.

Consider the following men and women, their circumstances and sin, and be amazed with me at what God made of them.

Jacob was a lying schemer.	He was blessed by God and became the father of the Israelite nation.
Moses was a murderer, social dropout, and reclusive shepherd.	He was chosen by God to lead Israel from bondage in Egypt. He authored the first five books of the Bible.
Samson was a quick-tempered strongman who couldn't control his sexual appetites.	He was chosen by God as a judge of Israel and is listed in "Faith's Hall of Fame" in Hebrews 11.
Rahab was a prostitute.	God used her to protect Israel and made her part of the lineage of Christ.
David betrayed a loyal servant and committed adultery and murder.	He was God's choice to be king of Israel and wrote many psalms.
Jonah was a bigot who refused to offer grace to his enemies and refused a direct order from God.	God used him as His spokesman in the greatest revival outside Israel in Old Testament history.
Matthew was a despised tax collector who took advantage of his own people to earn a buck.	He became a disciple and author of the Gospel of Matthew.

continued

Peter was an impetuous, uneducated fisherman who denied Christ.	He became the leader of the disciples and wrote two books of the Bible.
Paul was a murderer and persecutor of early Christians.	He became the greatest missionary and theologian of the early church and wrote thirteen books of the New Testament.
John Mark was a coward, deserting Paul when things got tough.	He became a helper to Paul and Peter and wrote the Gospel of Mark.

The evidence is overwhelming, especially to someone whose dream has died. God can use each one of us. God can do this because He is great and awesome.

"Never will I leave you;
never will I forsake you."

So we say with confidence,

"The Lord is my helper; I will not be afraid.
What can man do to me?" (Hebrews 13:5-6)

• •

Life is a grindstone. But whether it grinds us down or polishes us up depends on us.

—L. THOMAS HOLDCROFT

Get a Grip on Reality

Although we should never expect our dreams to fail, we really shouldn't be surprised when bad things happen. God didn't promise that all of our dreams will come true. If they did, we'd be the first

211

in history to have that happen. We live in a fallen world dominated by evil. By His grace, God restrains but does not contain evil's influence on earth. To expect Him to shelter us from every storm would be to expect more than Jesus experienced.

> *Dear friends, do not be surprised at the painful trial you are suffering, as though something strange were happening to you. But rejoice that you participate in the sufferings of Christ, so that you may be overjoyed when his glory is revealed. (1 Peter 4:12-13)*

Growth Op

Put yourself and your own failed dreams in a two-column format like the one on pages 208-209. What has God done that enables you to fill in the second column?

Every life has some sorrow and suffering in it. No exceptions. Just that small realization can help a lot when we're feeling like God has somehow singled us out for adversity. We've all heard about the man who complained because he had no shoes, until he met the man who had no feet. There's a lot of usable daily truth to that old story. When we're feeling sorry for ourselves, all we have to do is look around. There's always someone else worse off. When we're feeling mistreated, all we have to do is pick up the New Testament and read of the greatest mistreatment of all time.

Deal with the Sin

Of the possible failures that might checker our past and end or delay our dreams, few could be as dramatic as David's. Falling in lust with Bathsheba, he committed adultery, fathered an illegitimate child, and then murdered her husband, a loyal servant, to cover it up. If what you did was worse than that, I guess you have a right to get depressed. But I doubt many will qualify.

When David came face-to-face with his sin, courtesy of Nathan the prophet, he confessed his sin and pled for mercy from God. His testimony in Psalm 51 remains a classic of a repentant heart.

Have mercy on me, O God,
according to your unfailing love;
according to your great compassion
blot out my transgressions.
Wash away all my iniquity
and cleanse me from my sin.

For I know my transgressions,
and my sin is always before me.
Against you, you only, have I sinned
and done what is evil in your sight,
so that you are proved right when you speak
and justified when you judge. (Psalm 51:1-4)

There is no blame, no self-justification, just a man naked with his sin before a holy but merciful God. David honestly faced his moral failure, just as we must. Confession is crucial for the Christian. The apostle John reminds us,

But if we walk in the light, as he is in the light, we have
fellowship with one another, and the blood of Jesus, his
Son, purifies us from all sin.
If we claim to be without sin, we deceive ourselves
and the truth is not in us. If we confess our sins, he is
faithful and just and will forgive us our sins and purify
us from all unrighteousness. If we claim we have not
sinned, we make him out to be a liar and his word has
no place in our lives. (1 John 1:7-10)

If even a small portion of the failure of your dream rests on your moral failure before God, you must bring it before Him. To cover it, to remain proud, will bring more trouble.

He who conceals his sins does not prosper,
but whoever confesses and renounces them
finds mercy.

Blessed is the man who always fears the LORD,
but he who hardens his heart falls into trouble.
(Proverbs 28:13-14)

· ·

He is a wise man who does not grieve for the things which he has not, but rejoices for those which he has.

—EPICTETUS,
GREEK PHILOSOPHER (A.D. 55–135)

GrowthOp

Make a list of the little blessings in your life from just the last week. If none come to mind, ask yourself some questions: Has your car been running smoothly? Do you have hot water for a shower? Has someone told you that he or she cares? Do you have clothes to wear? Has a coworker complimented you? Is your roof not leaking? If it is, is it only leaking in three spots? Have you been able to make progress on a project? Has your child come home with a good grade? You get the idea.

If the failure of your dream has anything to do with your unfaithfulness, the best thing you can do is to be faithful in the small things.

If God has forgiven you, to refuse to forgive yourself or others is the height of arrogance. In our own life as husband and wife, we're still on a steep learning curve about this. When we fail to forgive each other and let even little hurts build up, we begin to harbor resentment, which grows into anger. Pretty soon we've built a wall between the two of us and between each of us and God. Plus, we "fall into trouble," as Proverbs says in various areas. In a practical sense, thinking clearly when writing a book together becomes nearly impossible when we don't forgive each other and ourselves for not being perfect. Once we forgave each other for some past offenses, the walls came down. After love and forgiveness, our work began to flow freely again. This certainly isn't the first time our unforgiveness has caused us to fall into trouble, nor, I'm sure, will it be the last. But we know what to do about it when it does.

Focus on the Little Things in Your Life, and Celebrate God's Goodness to You

When things go wrong, when we're hard up against failure, it's so easy

214

to forget the small blessings that God brings us every day. It's also easy to consider the mundane parts of life as insignificant. If we've learned anything, it's that they're not.

••

Lord, help me do great things as though they were little, since I do them with Your powers; and help me to do little things as though they were great, because I do them in Your Name.

—BLAISE PASCAL, FRENCH MATHEMATICIAN AND PHILOSOPHER (1623–1662)

Don't Isolate—Do Circulate

When we feel like a failure, sometimes the last thing we want to do is be around other people. What may feel more comfortable for a while is very self-destructive in the long run. God did not create us to live detached from one another. Isolation only serves to reinforce depression and despair for most people. Anyone who has lost a dream knows the value of a few friends who are willing to bear one another's burdens. The apostle Paul reminds us, "Carry each other's burdens, and in this way you will fulfill the law of Christ" (Galatians 6:2).

We need each other not only for support, but also for stimulation. The chances of a renewed vision drop proportionately to the degree of isolation we choose. Continued isolation causes our world and our sense of reality to shrink dramatically. That's why we're encouraged to get together with other men and women who love Christ.

Growth Op

It's harder to get into circulation when we don't feel like it. The same principle works for this as for blessings. Start small. Invite a trusted confidant to coffee. Share your pain over your dream with him or her. Two heads, as they say, are better than one. He or she may point out something you missed. Maybe a new door of opportunity will open up. Maybe you'll get some loving feedback about your part in the failure of a dream. Or maybe you'll just feel better for having shared your burden.

And let us consider how we may spur one another on toward love and good deeds. Let us not give up meeting together, as some are in the habit of doing, but let us encourage one another — and all the more as you see the Day approaching. (Hebrews 10:24-25)

Never Give Up

After the heroic days of World War II, when life had slowed down for Winston Churchill, he was asked to speak at Sandhurst, his alma mater. Churchill, who had been quite a failure at that school, must have found the headmaster's introduction humorous. To the auditorium full of schoolboys, he said, "Young men, be sure you take copious notes, because this will probably be one of the greatest speeches you'll ever hear." It's doubtful many students took notes, but it was one of the most unforgettable speeches of all time. Churchill rose to the podium and said, "Never give up."

After a minute's pause, he continued even more boldly.

"NEVER give up!"

Which was followed by another lengthy pause. And then, pounding his fist on the podium, he shouted at the top of his lungs:

"Never,

"Never,

"Never,

"Never,

"NEVER GIVE UP!"

And then he turned and quietly sat down.[1]

Of course, Churchill knew what he was talking about when he gave that speech. He'd experienced major failure twice in his public life. Even when he left public life for a number of years, he warned England of the threat of Nazi Germany. But no one paid attention to a political outcast; that is, until 1940, when at age sixty-five he was asked to replace Neville Chamberlain as prime minister. With his stubborn courage, he led the British people and the democratic Western world from the brink of defeat to a final victory in the greatest conflict the world has ever seen.

Make Yourself Available to God

Remembering who God is, getting a grip on reality, dealing with sin, focusing on the little things in life, getting back into circulation—all are part of the process of building on the ashes when dreams die. And all are also ways to make ourselves available to God. We'd like to bring up one more. Earlier in the book we devoted a whole chapter to prayer. In other places in this book, we talk about getting to know God, which, of course, like developing any other relationship, takes time. Only one person is going to be able to answer your deepest questions and doubts about why your dream did not succeed. That person is God. Don't abandon Him now. Pray, pray, and pray.

Growth Op

When a dream fails, we can take it as a sign we're worthless or we can take ourselves to God, saying, "Here I am, ready for Your next open door in my life."

18

How to Keep a Dream Alive

Adversity is sometimes hard upon a man; but for one man who can stand prosperity, there are a hundred that will stand adversity.

THOMAS CARLYLE, SCOTTISH ESSAYIST AND HISTORIAN (1795–1881)

Life is meant to bring a succession of discoveries of our need of Christ, and with every discovery the way is open for a new inflow of the supply.

MILES J. STANFORD

Times were tough in fifth-century Jerusalem. They were tough in the Depression. And, come to think of it, they're tough today. Any time in history can seem like the worst of times if we're living in it. Because of the problems that plague our fallen world, it's never easy to keep a dream alive. Just because we have a good beginning doesn't ensure that we'll finish strong. The ability to make wise decisions daily is as crucial in the middle and mature stages of a dream as at its inception. And if we fail to make wise choices — even seemingly insignificant, everyday choices — we can place our dream in jeopardy. As we've seen again and again throughout this book, prayer and a vibrant relationship with God inform these choices, guiding us to wisdom.

> First we make our decisions, and then our decisions make us.
>
> —HOWARD HENDRICKS,
> AMERICAN THEOLOGIAN

We can't understand all of God's workings, but if our purpose is indeed His purpose, we can assume He wants us to succeed with our dream. We can also assume that He wants us to draw on His wisdom to make choices that contribute to the dream's continued life. Because Nehemiah acted wisely, his dream lived through the most threatening circumstances.

Hard Times in Jerusalem

Though they had not given up their verbal barrages, Jerusalem's enemies were no longer a physical threat. The fulfillment of the dream was in sight. The work was progressing on the walls at a rapid pace. Success was in view. But it wasn't a time to relax. All was going well until "the men and their wives raised a great outcry against their Jewish brothers" (Nehemiah 5:1).

The word *great* here indicates a bitter, boisterous cry of distress. This was not whimpering by a few whiners, but a demonstrative complaint by a considerable group of people. What was their problem? Nehemiah 5:2-5 outlines their complaint. Life was rough. Some were mortgaging their fields to eat. Others had to borrow money to pay taxes. Still others with no money, property, or collateral were indenturing their children so they could eat.

It's not a surprise—a large number of people were just getting by. Their life in the construction gang made things even more difficult, and now there was a famine to boot. Even when everyone is hurting, it seems there is always someone who's able to make a buck out of the situation. Many people made their fortunes during the Great Depression. Those who found themselves in a cash position were able to pick up property at dirt-cheap prices. Poor farmers who needed to feed their families had no choice but to sell. Sadly, rather than helping, many wealthy people got wealthier at someone else's expense. The same sort of thing was happening in Jerusalem. And it threatened to kill Nehemiah's dream.

As we read this story, we notice that Nehemiah used seven wise strategies that kept his dream alive during this crisis.

• •

No man can become rich without himself enriching others.

—ANDREW CARNEGIE,
SCOTTISH-BORN INDUSTRIALIST AND PHILANTHROPIST

If you pay peanuts, you get monkeys.

—ANONYMOUS

Be Generous with People

Let greed be our prime motive, fail to be generous with people, and we are putting nails in the coffin of our dream. People on the take are destined to ultimate failure. If getting all we can at the expense of others is driving our dream, we can be sure we'll not only come up empty but end up on the backside of God as well. The apostle Paul made it clear. Greed is the quickest way to pain. "Some people, eager for money, have wandered from the faith and pierced themselves with many griefs" (1 Timothy 6:10).

On the other hand, the way to be truly rich is taking the path of generosity.

> *Command them to do good, to be rich in good deeds, and to be generous and willing to share. In this way they will lay up treasure for themselves as a firm foundation for the coming age, so that they may take hold of the life that is truly life. (1 Timothy 6:18-19)*

Even though some of his peers were making a bundle, Nehemiah resisted the temptation to get rich at his people's expense. Although it would have been possible for him to become fabulously wealthy, it cost too much if it meant taking advantage of others. He was obviously a giver rather than a taker. In fact, he gave more than was expected.

> *Instead, I devoted myself to the work on this wall. All my men were assembled there for the work; we did not acquire any land.*
>
> *Furthermore, a hundred and fifty Jews and officials ate at my table, as well as those who came to us from the surrounding nations. Each day one ox, six choice sheep and some poultry were prepared for me, and every ten days an abundant supply of wine of all kinds. In spite of all this, I never demanded the food allotted to the governor, because the demands were heavy on these people.*
>
> *Remember me with favor, O my God, for all I have done for these people. (Nehemiah 5:16-19)*

A Tale of Two Organizations

Consider two situations. The first is a corporation that consistently faces financial shortfalls. The men and women in the field are proverbially expected to do more with less. Words of appreciation for sacrifice are almost nonexistent — after all, they're only doing their jobs. In fact, upper-level management is suspicious that employees are really wasting resources, so they keep a close eye on expense reports. Raises are infrequent and come with a curt "This is all we could do"; never "You people are the greatest, we wish we could do more." The messages, verbal and nonverbal, emphasize that employees are fortunate to work with such a great corporation. Is it any wonder their employees feel used, job satisfaction is low, and performance deteriorates every year?

The second organization faces similar cash-flow problems. In fact, employee salaries are no better than at the first. But what may be lacking in cash is made up in appreciation. Every memo reminds people how valuable they are to the organization. Every budget-trimming measure comes with an apology—"We are so sorry we have to do this to you." Every sacrifice gets a sincere thank you, and even small achievements are celebrated. When there were no raises last year, employees were sad, but there was no grumbling, just a determination to work harder for the success of the company so that next year they could get the raise they knew the owners of the company wanted to give them. And talk about performance— when an important project got cut, several employees got together and worked nights for three months (without pay) to get things back on schedule.

• •

Tell them to go after God, who piles on all the riches we could ever manage—to do good, to be rich in helping others, to be extravagantly generous.

—THE APOSTLE PAUL, 1 TIMOTHY 6:18, MSG

Most people aren't appreciated enough, and the bravest things we do in our lives are usually known only to ourselves. No one throws ticker tape on the man who chose to be faithful to his wife, on the lawyer who didn't take the drug money, or the daughter who held her tongue again and again.

—PEGGY NOONAN, PRESIDENTIAL SPEECH WRITER (B. 1952)

Growth Op

No matter how generous we are, there's probably not a person alive who couldn't be more generous. Make a list of ways you can open up your "emotional" or literal wallet and give to others. Some examples: Compliment my employees for their ordinary jobs well done. Offer to take over chores for my spouse so he or she can do something renewing. Tell my children how smart they are. Give a deserving employee a bonus if I can't afford a raise. Throw an appreciation dinner for volunteers who helped make a committee project work.

Which organization appears greedy? Which values its people? No question. What *is* a wonder, however, is that the first company is a Christian organization and the second is a "secular" company. What does it say about our beliefs and motives when secular companies outdo Christian companies in valuing their people? It says they are operating more biblically.

If we want people to give themselves to our dream, they have to know in no uncertain terms that we are here to serve, not to be served.

Listen, Stay in Touch

The second crucial strategy Nehemiah used to keep his dream alive was good communication. Absentee leadership doesn't work when you're building a dream. Neither will emotional absenteeism. Two-way communication is essential to any group effort. This means talking *and* listening. You can't possibly know what's going on if you can't or don't listen to those around you. If Nehemiah had not heard the complaint, what do you think would have happened? More than likely, at the very least, the work would have come to a standstill. But the fact is, Nehemiah was there, in touch, working with and listening to the people who worked for his cause.

If *A* is a success in life, then *A* equals *x* plus *y* plus *z*. Work is *x*; *y* is play; and *z* is keeping your mouth shut.

—ALBERT EINSTEIN

Interestingly, it's also possible to isolate ourselves from what's going on by refusing to deal with reality — "Oh, that wouldn't happen to me." One of the most colossal denials the world has ever known was British prime minister Neville Chamberlain's belief that Hitler wasn't interested in controlling Europe—that giving him Czechoslovakia would ensure peace.

Growth Op

When is the last time you stopped to listen? To your spouse? Children? Parents? Employees? Friends? Yourself? Hint: If you can't remember, it's probably been too long.

As hard as some things might be to stomach, we must listen and be cognizant of what's going on around us if we don't want our dreams to die right before our eyes.

Nehemiah certainly listened, even though the information was unpleasant. He was alert. He knew the people's pain and hardships firsthand, and he took steps to help them personally. He listened, probed behind what was said, and found out that the real problem was not poverty, but usury.

Manage Anger Before It Controls You

We use the word *manage* because, without a doubt, anger is one of the most powerful emotions we experience, and it needs to be managed if we are to keep our dream alive. Out of control, it is deadly to us as well as to our dream. It may make us feel better to vent on someone, but at what price?

> How much more grievous are the consequences of anger than the causes of it.
>
> —MARCUS AURELIUS, ROMAN EMPEROR (A.D. 121–180)

Nehemiah provides an excellent example of handling anger. Although he was "very angry," he was able to channel his anger for positive results. He gives us a threefold technique for handling anger in a wise and purposeful way.

> *When I heard their outcry and these charges, I was very angry. I pondered them in my mind and then accused*

the nobles and officials. I told them, "You are exacting usury from your own countrymen!" So I called together a large meeting to deal with them. (Nehemiah 5:6-7)

Read Ephesians 4:26-32. What insights do you see in this passage about handling anger?

First, notice that Nehemiah admitted his anger to himself. He didn't excuse it, ignore it, repress it, or minimize it. He was mad. What the nobles were doing to the poorer Jews was reprehensible.

Second, he pondered the situation. Anger must always be evaluated. Is our anger justified? If so, how should it be handled? Yes, we can always express it to God, but what about others? Will it harm or help them?

Third, Nehemiah took action. When he knew his anger was legitimate and under control, when he knew how to express it in a productive way, he confronted the nobles, first privately, and then publicly.

Confront People Problems

Okay, we confess. We both hate conflict and confrontation. But if we ignore people problems, hoping they will go away, we put our dreams in great danger.

••

Brothers, if someone is caught in a sin, you who are spiritual should restore him gently. But watch yourself, or you also may be tempted.

—THE APOSTLE PAUL, GALATIANS 6:1

Sometimes people do and say things that need to be confronted. Yes, Jesus warned us, "Do not judge, or you will be judged." Loose criticism does a great deal of damage. But Jesus also taught:

If your brother sins against you, go and show him his fault, just between the two of you. If he listens to you, you have won your brother over. But if he will not listen, take one or two others along, so that "every matter may be established by the testimony of two or three witnesses." If he refuses to listen to them, tell it to the church; and if he refuses to listen even to the church, treat him as you would a pagan or a tax collector. (Matthew 18:15-17)

As long as there are people, there will be people problems. And as long as we dream, we need people. The cost of confrontation is often high. But the cost of neglect is even higher. This was probably one of Nehemiah's most difficult tasks.

I pondered [the charges] in my mind and then accused the nobles and officials. I told them, "You are exacting usury from your own countrymen!" So I called together a large meeting to deal with them and said: "As far as possible, we have bought back our Jewish brothers who were sold to the Gentiles. Now you are selling your brothers, only for them to be sold back to us!" They kept quiet, because they could find nothing to say.

So I continued, "What you are doing is not right. Shouldn't you walk in the fear of our God to avoid the reproach of our Gentile enemies? I and my brothers and my men are also lending the people money and grain. But let the exacting of usury stop! Give back to them immediately their fields, vineyards, olive groves and houses, and also the usury you are charging them — the hundredth part of the money, grain, new wine and oil."

"We will give it back," they said. "And we will not demand anything more from them. We will do as you say."

Then I summoned the priests and made the nobles and officials take an oath to do what they had promised.

I also shook out the folds of my robe and said, "In this way may God shake out of his house and possessions every man who does not keep this promise. So may such a man be shaken out and emptied!"

At this the whole assembly said, "Amen," and praised the LORD. And the people did as they had promised. (Nehemiah 5:7-13)

When we decide that we need to confront someone, the first thing to do is to stop and think. What behavior are we criticizing? What changes need to be made? If you are culpable in any way for the situation, sometimes it's a good idea to start with that. For instance, perhaps you haven't made it entirely clear what you expect.

Explain clearly and calmly what behavior is unacceptable. Never attack the person, only the sin or failing. This seems like such an obvious principle, but sometimes it's hard to hold on to. Who among us hasn't accused our spouse of being an insensitive person, rather than specifying the behavior that made us feel uncared for?

Give the person you are confronting a chance to respond. Perhaps there are extenuating circumstances you don't know about. This is a good time to listen. However, if all you're hearing is excuses — or victimization — gently and clearly point that out.

Try to arrive at a mutual plan for correcting the situation. Be clear about what the consequences are. If your child doesn't pick up his toys, will you confiscate them for a week? If your employee doesn't meet your standards, will she be put on probation? Will she be let go?

Think of a time you confronted someone in the heat of the moment. Go back over that conversation and rewrite it, keeping Nehemiah's story in mind. If it's possible, go to that person and rework through the confrontation using your new scenario.

Set Fair Standards That Apply to Everyone

Most people can tolerate even tough leadership when they know that "everyone is in this thing together." For example, there was probably never a tougher general than Douglas MacArthur, and yet he was adored by the men who served under him. Why? Because the stars on his shoulder didn't keep him from sharing the same dangers and discomforts that he asked his beloved men to endure. Nehemiah followed the same strategy, as we see in 5:14:

> The LORD abhors dishonest scales, but accurate weights are his delight.
>
> —PROVERBS 11:1

> *Moreover, from the twentieth year of King Artaxerxes, when I was appointed to be their governor in the land of Judah, until his thirty-second year—twelve years— neither I nor my brothers ate the food allotted to the governor.*

The same principle applies at home. Double standards simply won't fly. If family rules are simply for the convenience of parents and don't apply to everyone, then we can expect rebellion.

Class systems are not only demoralizing, they are unbiblical. According to Paul, we're all in this together—equally valuable. We owe each other a great degree of respect:

 **GrowthOp**

Write down five fair standards you expect others to live by. Now rewrite the same list saying how you expect to live by them as well.

> *There should be no division in the body, . . . its parts should have equal concern for each other. If one part suffers, every part suffers with it; if one part is honored, every part rejoices with it. (1 Corinthians 12:25-26)*

Focus on Being a Servant Rather Than a Celebrity

God assays our lives in two dramatic ways: in adversity and in prosperity. It's easy to see how adversity tests our metal, but we usually don't think about success as a test. But success has upset the

• •

No person is ever on trial so much as at the moment of excessive good fortune.

—LEW WALLACE,
BEN HUR (1880) (1827–1905)

equilibrium for many a good man and woman, as well as ended some wonderful dreams. The work ethic, motive, and camaraderie that made the dream so compelling often change dramatically when the dreamer suddenly finds himself or herself beginning to look out over the landscape of success. Fighting off external adversaries is one thing, but when success comes, a whole nest of vipers is born that could kill or cripple our dream. The worst snake in the pit is the belief that we are now somehow better than someone else.

Christ didn't leave room for speculation on the issue of greatness.

Think of something you can do to be a servant to those you lead, and do it. This could be taking that contract your assistant worked overtime on to Federal Express yourself. It could be sitting with your son as he studies for a math test or taking your daughter to the park instead of golfing on Saturday morning.

Whoever wants to become great among you must be your servant, and whoever wants to be first must be slave of all. For even the Son of Man did not come to be served, but to serve, and to give his life as a ransom for many. (Mark 10:43–45)

Let's be clear: being a servant of people is first and foremost a matter of obedience to God. When we live on the take or allow a predatory corporate culture to dominate the thinking of those who work with us, we can expect God's discipline in our lives. God requires those in authority to be just and generous with those who work for or with them. There is a very pragmatic side to this as well. A "you're here to serve me" mentality among leaders is the quickest way to ensure poor morale and mediocre work from everyone in an organization. Only a servant can bring out the best in people.

Keep the Main Thing the Main Thing

In other words, stay off rabbit trails. The focus that brought you to this stage of your dream can't be surrendered if you want to keep that dream alive. We're not saying that balance is not important. That's assumed. But companies, organizations, churches, and families that forget their purpose are in danger of losing their dream. Nehemiah handled well the invitation to hunt rabbits in chapter 6. He knew he was there to build, not to get involved in summit diplomacy.

> Perfection of means and confusion of goals seem—in my opinion—to characterize our age.
>
> —ALBERT EINSTEIN

> *"I am carrying on a great project and cannot go down. Why should the work stop while I leave it and go down to you?" Four times they sent me the same message, and each time I gave them the same answer. (Nehemiah 6:3-4)*

It's not that peace with his neighbors was not important, but Nehemiah didn't have time to solve all the problems of the world. There would be time for that later. Right then, in Nehemiah's life, the focus was building. That's what he stuck to.

Whether it's intimidation, as it was in Nehemiah's case, or temptation that lures us away from our purpose, we must recognize it for what it is: a rabbit trail.

Growth Op

One of the biggest temptations leading us away from our dream is the lure of worldly success. If we have a successful business providing a much-needed service and a chance to expand into three other kinds of service, it might be an opportunity. Or it might be a blind alley. While we're not negating our earlier advice to dream big, the same questions that applied to the initial dream should apply to the expansion. Plus, it's probably even more important to ponder, plan, and pray—especially pray—this time through. Pride being what it is, we're sometimes tempted to let our reach exceed our grasp when we have some success under our belt. Will taking on the new endeavor undermine what good work we're already doing? Will we be spread too thin? Will we divert much-needed resources from our core project?

19

Becoming a Dream Builder

An unfulfilled vocation drains the colour from a man's entire existence.

HONORÉ DE BALZAC, FRENCH NOVELIST (1799–1850)

People influence people.

ROBERT MAGER

"**B**illy, can you tell us the answer?" I couldn't, of course, because once again I'd been in a faraway world, heroically saving the day in the usual way second graders do. "Billy, you've got to pay attention." "Yes ma'am," I always dutifully replied, resolving to in my childlike way, but then, something would happen and I'd find myself daydreaming about killing Martians. Much to the consternation of my appointed mentors (a.k.a. parents), "Tends to daydream" appeared more than once on my report card in those early years. In my opinion, daydreaming about the future was a lot more interesting than the present reality of math, grammar, geography, spelling, and history. Eventually, I learned to practice the painful discipline of keeping my mind focused in the present. Unfortunately, I learned that lesson all too well.

Schools, teachers, and parents must walk a fine line on this one. Yes, it's important to teach our children to keep on task, and to let them know that sometimes learning the things they need to know requires mundane grunt work. Too often, kids daydream because school is mind-numbingly dull. But it's also important to foster and encourage daydreams. And, as we said, it is those childhood dreams, when encouraged but not allowed to grow out of hand, that can teach us the skills to be able to dream life-changing dreams later in life. We believe that even children can have dreams from God. So we'd better be careful how we chastise daydreamers.

Some years back I remember reading the account of a young boy who heard a radio news report about homeless people in his hometown. This was a young man with a daydream and parents who understood what it was to dream. So when he announced that he wanted to take his extra blanket and some food to these people, his father took him in the family car. As these things do, his dream grew and soon there were

Have you ever squelched a child's dream? Perhaps you should apologize and ask God to help you be a dream builder rather than a dream buster.

many people joining in his effort to feed, clothe, and shelter homeless people. What would have happened if this young man's father had said, "Oh, Son, I'm sorry. But there are so many homeless people, there's really nothing we can do about it"?

People who dream are essential for any family, organization, church, business, city, and country. In fact, dreaming is important for every single human being. But how are we going to produce adults who dream if we squelch every dream a child has?

Sometimes it's through mistakes that we can teach the difference between good dreams and selfish ones. A mother told us of her young daughter who had strong entrepreneurial instincts and was always dreaming up new businesses—age-appropriate, of course, but quite creative. She offered to check coats at her parents' annual Christmas party for all of their acquaintances and business associates. Thinking her daughter was being responsible and glad for the offer of help, her mother agreed—only to discover after about thirty guests had arrived that the girl was charging them a dollar apiece to check their coats. Never one to miss a teaching opportunity, this mother took a minute in the midst of her party to explain how a private party in their home is not like a trip to a museum or restaurant. She even praised her daughter

> I do not believe in a child's world. It is a fantasy world. I believe a child should be taught from the very first that the whole world is his world, that adults and children share one world, that all generations are needed.
>
> —PEARL BUCK, MISSIONARY TO CHINA AND PULITZER PRIZE WINNER

for her creativity and initiative but stressed what a breach of hospitality she had committed. The daughter apologized to the individuals and gave their money back.

Stay Involved

As far as our own family goes, we're far from perfect. But we have to tell you that as we write this book we are acutely aware that it is an indescribable blessing to be part of a family of people who encourage each other to dream and move toward fulfilling the purpose for which God created them. As a matter of fact, that is part of our family mission—to help each other become all that we were created to be. This means creating an atmosphere where dreaming is encouraged. Though we can't make our kids dream or even prevent them from dreaming, we can make it immeasurably easier or harder for them to reach for all they were created to be.

All of us have the choice to be dream builders or dream busters in the lives of those around us. We haven't met any parents yet (ourselves included) who haven't been tempted at least to try to mold their kids into someone or something *they* think they should be. It takes parents with a strong sense of self-worth to recognize and communicate to their children that they are uniquely valuable and that God has created them for a special purpose—and that they want to help them discover it. It's all too easy to take our cues from culture—and fall into the trap of pushing our children into things that are supposedly the "right" things to do or be involved in, failing to consider their unique makeup and the dreams budding within them.

But we can't blame culture totally for pressuring our children to perform a certain way, be involved in certain activities, or choose certain professions. If we were honest we'd probably admit that at least sometimes we entertain thoughts of wanting to show off our children and say, "Look what I did!" And probably many of us should confess that we secretly dream that at least one of our children will become a record-breaking Olympic athlete, head of a multinational corporation, a senator, or maybe even president of the United States.

Don't get me wrong. Dreaming grand dreams for our children is fine as long as we honor God's design in each child. And this means we must be a student of each of our children and honor the dreams that are within them. Before we understood this, we created a lot of miserable moments—for the parents and the child—trying to squeeze John, our firstborn son, into a mold of our own making. For example, we dreamed about him playing the piano some day in Carnegie Hall. So we enrolled him in preschool music at a local university and private piano lessons. Many an afternoon was ruined as he tried to like this pursuit that was so important to his parents. God didn't create John to be a musician. He didn't give him excessive amounts of musical talent. It's not surprising then that John never dreamed dreams about being on stage performing. But God did give John incredible artistic skills, a whizlike ability on the computer, and an entrepreneurial spirit. So does John dream about his own graphic arts company? You bet he does. Has John already started a small such company while still in college? Of course he has. He's following the dreams within him, and we're trying to do everything we can to help.

> Allow children to be happy in their own way, for what better way will they ever find?
>
> —SAMUEL JOHNSON, ENGLISH AUTHOR (1709–1784)

A great debate continues to rage over what determines who we are. Some experts argue for the environment we grew up in as the most significant factor that shapes us. Others strongly believe it's our education—or lack of same. Still others say our emotional needs make us what we are. But these theories all begin from the same premise: They assume we are shapeless and blank when we arrive on the delivery table—like clay to be molded by the circumstances of life.

With this mind-set, we also believe—when we become adults—we can become whatever society pressures us to be, our family needs us to be, the church recruits us to be, our friends encourage us to be, our company promotes us to be, or in some instances, whatever the government determines we should be.

Certainly all of these factors influence us. However, they don't explain why we're all so different—why two children raised in the same home, by the same parents, with the same privileges, turn out so completely different.

The Bible, however, is very clear on this issue. The consistent statement of God's Word is that rather than being a shapeless mass of human potential, each one of us came with a prior design. We are not *becoming* someone—we *are* someone. Our distinctives are not the result of random selection or cultural and societal influences. We were created by a purposeful God who made us in His own image.

237

Then God said, "Let us make man in our image, in our
likeness, and let them rule over the fish of the sea and
the birds of the air, over the livestock, over all the earth,
and over all the creatures that move along the ground."
(Genesis 1:26)

Furthermore, God personally designed the detailed uniqueness
of every individual.

For you created my inmost being;
* you knit me together in my mother's womb.*
I praise you because I am fearfully and wonderfully
*   made;*
* your works are wonderful,*
* I know that full well.*
My frame was not hidden from you
* when I was made in the secret place.*
When I was woven together in the depths of the earth,
* your eyes saw my unformed body.*
All the days ordained for me
* were written in your book*
* before one of them came to be. (Psalm 139:13-16)*

We've often marveled at the fact that there are 60 billion different fingerprints currently in use. And amazingly, we can still expect
the next baby born to have ten new, totally unique prints of his or
her own.

How do our bodies know what to look like? A single human chromosome contains about 20 billion bits of information. This is the
equivalent of about 3.3 billion alphanumeric characters. If the aver-
age word contains six letters, the amount of information contained
in a chromosome is equivalent to 5.5 million words. If we assume
there are three hundred words to a page and five hundred pages to
a volume, then there are 3,704 volumes of information contained
in one single human chromosome. Multiply that number by forty-
eight chromosomes per cell and we learn that we have a stagger-

ing 177,777 volumes of information written on each cell of our bodies. Truly we are fearfully and wonderfully made. But that's only half the story.

If God goes to that much trouble with our physical body, what does this say about our complex "inmost being"—our mind, will, emotions, and dreams? Our basic strengths, abilities, and motivations are not "acquired" any more than blue eyes, curly hair, or long fingers are. They too are part of the great Designer's handiwork. What's more, nothing is arbitrary. There is purpose behind every detail. When God made us, He had something specific in mind for us to do, just as He had for Jeremiah.

The word of the LORD came to me, saying,

"Before I formed you in the womb I knew you,
*   before you were born I set you apart;*
*   I appointed you as a prophet to the nations."*
*   (Jeremiah 1:4-5)*

This verse should make us stop in our tracks. Rather than asking who we want our children to become, we need to ask who God has already made them to be, what dreams He has planted within them and how we can help nurture those dreams. That's not to say that they don't need to develop and mature. It simply means our children are not ours to shape. They are ours to nurture—according to their design. I can't change a child's design any more than I can make an oak tree into a maple. I can, however, nurture or stunt his or her growth.

As dream builders we're responsible for supporting the God-given dreams of not only our children, but our spouses as well. It's our job to help them become who God meant them to be. I would not be sitting at this computer writing this book right now if it weren't for the fact

> We can't form our children on our own concepts; we must take them and love them as God gives them to us.
>
> —JOHANN VON GOETHE, GERMAN POET (1749–1832)

that Bill is a committed dream builder. In chapter 4 we told the story of the retreat that changed my life. I consider it one of God's major gifts that my husband happened to be leading that particular retreat. Who knows? I might have gotten the message anyway. But, as it turned out, I not only got it from Bill, I got the unwavering support and loving criticism that helped my dream become reality. Unfortunately, we know husbands who discourage their wives from stepping out on a dream. And we know wives who throw cold water on their husbands' dreams.

Earlier in the book, we looked at the motives our critics have for thwarting our dreams. Sadly, those dream busters can be in our own family. Perhaps it's fear that their secure lives will be upset. Perhaps it's a sincere wish for their loved one not to be hurt. But we all need to remember that this life comes with ups and downs, bumps and bruises. We don't do our children, our spouses, or ourselves any favors when we literally or metaphorically try to keep the doors locked and ourselves safe inside, disengaged from the world. Before we ignore or attack a dream, we had better be sure we're not standing in God's way.

We can also help our friends pursue their dreams. I have a friend who sends me inspirational quotes that spur me on in the pursuit of my dreams. I have other friends with whom I brainstorm about how our God-given strengths and talents might open doors to let us pursue dreams none of us might have thought of on our own.

We can help anyone dream when we listen to his or her ideas and refuse to pour cold water on his or her visions of what could happen. Perhaps we help others most by pursuing our own God-given dreams. To be sure, dreamers are infectious. But there's more. When we follow God's dreams and see them become a reality, our action creates courage in others to dream God's dreams for themselves.

Because Nehemiah dreamed, prepared, prayed, planned, and persisted, Jerusalem had walls.

So the wall was completed on the twenty-fifth of Elul, in fifty-two days. When all our enemies heard about this, all the surrounding nations were afraid and lost their self-confidence, because they realized that this work had been done with the help of our God. (Nehemiah 6:15-16)

This feat was more than the fulfillment of a dream. It was more than a testimony of Nehemiah's leadership. It was even more than a demonstration of God's goodness. It was the beginning of hope for God's people. From behind those walls, they would be free to worship, free to rebuild their culture, and free to dream about the future. By following his dream, Nehemiah made it possible for millions of others to dream as well.

Because Nehemiah dreamed and Jerusalem was reestablished, the Jewish nation could once again prosper. More Jews would return and resettle towns like Bethany, Nazareth, and Bethlehem. They would raise their families knowing their children had a hope and a future. And when things were bleak, they would dream about the coming of Messiah. And when Messiah came, He brought the hope of ages within those sturdy walls—the dream that all men and women carry in their breast, the dream of being restored to their Creator. Nehemiah's was no insignificant dream. Neither is yours.

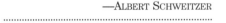

> Example is not the main thing in influencing others. It is the only thing.
>
> —ALBERT SCHWEITZER

Notes

Chapter Two: Set Apart—On Purpose
1. C. S. Lewis, *Mere Christianity* (New York: Macmillan, 1943), p. 174.

Chapter Six: Passion: Your Personal North Star
1. Richard C. Halverson, *Perspective*, 18 January 1978.

Chapter Eight: The Dawning of a Dream
1. Hugh Sidey, *TIME*, 17 November 1980.

Chapter Eleven: The Prayer Component
1. Benjamin Franklin, quoted by Robert Flood, ed., *The Rebirth of America* (Philadelphia: DeMoss Foundation, 1986), pg. 31.

Chapter Thirteen: The Waiting Game
1. *Links Letter* 16, no. 1, January–February 1996.

Chapter Fourteen: Is Your Vision Contagious?
1. J. Oswald Sanders, *Spiritual Leadership* (Chicago: Moody Press, 1980), p.202.
2. Winston Churchill, "Their Finest Hour," The Voice of Winston Churchill (recording), quoted in Richard H. Seume, *Nehemiah: God's Builder* (Chicago: Moody, 1978), p. 54.
3. Alan Loy McGinnis, *Bringing Out the Best in People* (Minneapolis: Augsburg, 1985), p. 93.
4. Abraham Lincoln, address given to the Washington Temperance Society, Springfield, Illinois, February 22, 1842.

Chapter Fifteen: Facing the Critics
1. David Houston, *Science Fiction Heroes* (New York: Knopf, 1994), p. 7.
2. Donald K. Campbell, *Nehemiah: Man in Charge* (Wheaton, Ill.: Victor, 1984), p. 39.

Chapter Seventeen: Building on the Ashes: When Dreams Die
1. Tim Hansel, *Holy Sweat* (Waco, Tex.: Word Books, 1987), p. 131.

Authors

WILLIAM CARR (BILL) PEEL is director of the Paul Tournier Institute of the Christian Medical and Dental Society, a discipleship ministry among health-care professionals. He is the co-creator of *The Saline Solution*, a board-certified continuing education program for physicians that teaches them how to share their faith in the context of a busy practice. Bill is also the president of Foundations for Living, a nonprofit organization committed to helping men and women discover how they can positively impact their world for Christ in the midst of everyday life—especially through their careers. He pioneered work with men in the 1970s and has been responsible for hundreds of men belonging to small groups.

In 1993, Bill was involved in a nationwide radio campaign calling men to prayer. Currently, he is a member of the Promise Keepers National Speakers Team. Bill teaches leadership seminars for corporations and travels frequently, speaking at churches and conferences. He has also been a popular guest on numerous television and radio programs.

Bill is the author of three books: the first Promise Keepers study guide, *What God Does When Men Pray* (NavPress/Promise Keepers, 1993), *Living in the Lion's Den Without Being Eaten* (NavPress 1994), and *Where Is Moses When We Need Him? Teaching Your Kids Ten Values That Matter Most* (Broadman & Holman, 1995).

Bill holds a B.A. from Southern Methodist University and a Th.M. from Dallas Theological Seminary.

KATHY PEEL is a nationally recognized family-management expert. She is the founder and president of The Family Manager™, a company committed to providing helpful ideas and resources to strengthen busy families and enhance the home. She has served as spokesperson for Hallmark Cards, Helene Curtis-Suave, Secret Adventures children's video series, and Entertainment with Values videos.

Kathy is a best-selling author of twelve books, which have sold over 1.2 million copies. She is the founder and editor-in-chief of *Family Manager* magazine, serves on the staff of *Family Circle* magazine, and writes regular columns for *Child*, *Aspire*, and *Release Ink* magazines. She has also been featured in numerous newspapers and magazines, including *Entrepreneur*, *Business Week*, *Working Mother*, *Kindred Spirit*, *Virtue*, *Parents of Teenagers*, *Decision*, and the cover of *Today's Christian Woman and Release Ink*.

Kathy has been a guest on over 350 TV and radio programs including *Good Morning America*, *CNN*, *The Home Show*, *Fox "After Breakfast"*, *Crook and Chase*, *RealLife*, *Focus on the Family* and *The Family Channel*. She speaks frequently, nationally and internationally, at conferences and conventions.

Kathy received a B.A. in 1972 from Southern Methodist University.

Bill and Kathy have three sons.

If you would like to inquire about Bill or Kathy Peel's speaking schedule, call Ambassadors Artist Agency at 615-370-4700.

If you would like to receive Kathy Peel's Family Manager Newsletter, please write:

The Family Manager
P.O. Box 50577
Nashville, TN 37205